THE VERSATILE TORTILLA COOKBOOK

A Terrier Book
Published by Easy Banana Press

Copyright © 1991 by Henry R. Lorenzo

ISBN 0-9613879-3-9

HENRY R. LORENZO

THE

VERSATILE TORTILLA

COOKBOOK

EASY BANANA PRODUCTIONS   SAN FRANCISCO

Charles R. Graham   Editor

1991

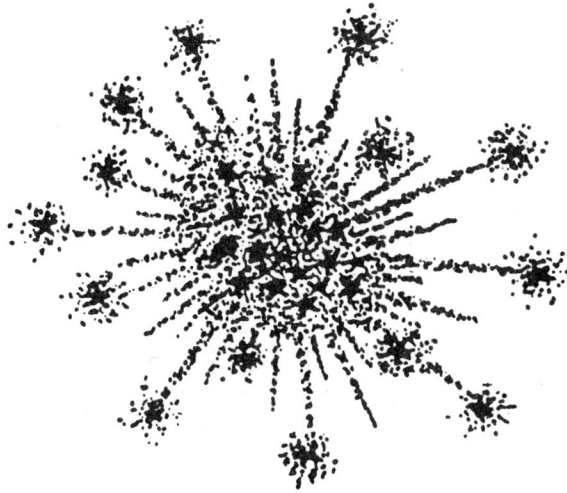

ACKNOWLEDGMENTS

To Jack Anderson for his professional advice and editing.
To Dick Graham for the technical execution of this endeavor.

DEDICATION

To David Gomez-Castró whose genius in the kitchen was the inspiration for this book.

To Cal Moore for sharing the culinary education at Chateau Montelén in Acalpulco for many seasons.

To Josh and Cheryl whose appreciation and support served as added inspiration.

To all the unsung *tortilleras* in Mexico and elsewhere.

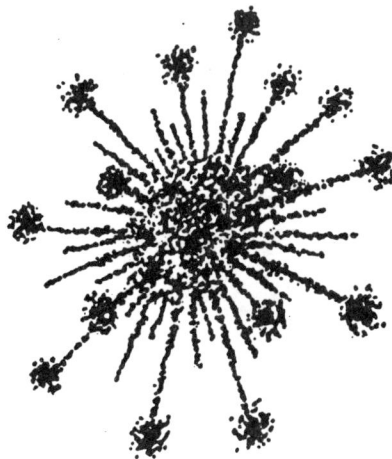

INTRODUCTION

The tortilla is one of the most versatile foods known to man. It is an ancient bread dating back to the Mayan civilization. The tortilla has virtually remained unchanged over the centuries. The sole ingredients for the tortilla is masa harina (corn meal), or wheat flour, and water - with perhaps a little salt.

When the Spanish conquistadores arrived in the New World in the early Sixteenth Century they gave the name tortilla to the thin pancake-like bread. It resembled, in shape and size the Spanish tortilla, which is an omelette of potatoes and eggs to which bits of vegetables and meats are sometimes added.

Originally, all tortillas were made from ground corn, the grain the Spaniards found in the New World. The corn was soaked in lime or ash and made into a dough. Today, corn tortillas are usually made from masa harina, a commercially dried corn flour. The Spanish conquistadores introduced wheat flour to the New World. Thus, the flour tortilla was developed.

The tortilla has remained, over the centuries, the fundamental and most important food in Mexico and Central American cuisine. Today, the tortilla continues to inspire California, Texas and Southwestern chefs to create new dishes and improve variations of the old. We salute the versatile tortilla.

CONTENTS

Casseroles and Baked Dishes 3

Traditional Enchiladas and Nouvelle Enchiladas 27

Classic Tacos, New Wave Tacos and Fajitas 45

Burritos 67

Quesadillas 77

Chilaquiles and Chimichangas 85

Tostadas and Tortas 93

Soups and Salads 101

Hors d'Oeuvres...111

Desserts 117

Tortillas 125

Helpful Hints 127

Glossary 129

Index 133

Casseroles

and

Baked Dishes

Tortilla-Chicken-Cheese Bake

1 onion, sliced
1 carrot, sliced
1 celery stalk, sliced
1 bay leaf
4 cloves garlic, minced or pressed
2 lb chicken breasts or thighs
1 can (7 oz) diced green chiles
1 can (16 oz) tomatillos (substitute cherry tomatoes if not available)
1 large onion, chopped
1/3 C cilantro, chopped
3 T vegetable oil
1 C reserved chicken stock
1 doz corn tortillas (6-7 in), cut in strips
3 C cooked rice (brown or white)
1 lb Monterey Jack cheese, grated
2 avocados, sliced (for garnish)
   prepared salsa

Bring 1 1/2 quarts water to boil with the onion, carrot, celery, bay leaf and 2 cloves of the garlic. Poach chicken until just tender (about 10 minutes) and drain, reserving 2 cups of the cooking stock and the cooked vegetables - remove the bay leaf. When cool enough to handle, bone and skin chicken and cut into bite-sized pieces. Sprinkle with salt and pepper. Pure the cooked vegetables.

Combine the chiles, tomatillos, the remaining two cloves of garlic and the cilantro in a food processor or blender. Blend until still chunky. Add the puréed vegetables and mix.

Heat oil in skillet and saut mixture for 5 minutes. Stir in chicken stock, gradually. Season to taste with salt and pepper. Fry tortillas in hot oil until just crisp and drain on paper towels.

Grease a 13 x 9 x 2 inch baking dish. Place a layer of 1/2 the tortillas, chicken, rice, sauted vegetable mixture, and cheese. Repeat layers ending with the grated cheese.

Bake at 350 for 40 minutes or until heated through and cheese is melted. Garnish with avocado slices and serve with your favorite salsa. Serves 8.

Chicken-Yogurt Enchilada Casserole

1 1/2 lb poached chicken breasts, recipe follows
(left over cooked chicken, cut into bite-sized cubes, may be used)
1/4 C butter or marjarine
1/4 C all-purpose flour
2 C poaching liquid (or regular strength chicken broth)
1 C unflavored yogurt
1 can (7 oz) diced green chiles
1 doz corn tortillas (6-7 in)
1 medium onion, chopped
1 lb Monterey Jack cheese, shredded
chile powder
1/3 C minced green onions (use part of green)

In 2 quart pan, melt butter over medium heat. Add flour and stir until bubbly. Whisk in poaching liquid or chicken broth - stir until it comes to a boil. Re- from heat. Mix in unflavored yogurt and chiles.

Cover bottom of a 9 x 13 x 2 inch baking dish with 1/3 of the sauce. Dip tortillas quickly in water - drain briefly and cut into 1 inch strips. Place 1/2 of the tor- tillas over the sauce. Cover evenly with all the chicken and chopped onion, 2/3 of the cheese and 1/3 of the sauce. Top with remaining tortillas, sauce and cheese. Dust top with chile powder.

Bake at 375 for 30 to 35 minutes until hot and bubbly in center. Sprinkle with green onions. Serves 8.

Poached Chicken Breasts

1 1/2 lb chicken breasts
1/4 t dried thyme
1/4 t rosemary
2 T instant chicken boullion
salt and pepper, to taste

1 large stalk celery, coarsely chopped
4 C water
1 medium carrot, coarsely chopped
1 small onion, coarsely chopped

Bring water to boil in medium-sized saucepan. Place chicken and remaining ingredients in water. Bring to a simmer, cover and simmer for 10 minutes. Re- move from heat and drain, reserving 2 cups broth. Remove skin and bones and discard. Cut meat into bite-sized chunks.

Chicken Breasts Montecito

3 T vegetable oil
6 corn tortillas (6-7 in)
2 C enchilada sauce
2 jalapeño peppers, seeded and chopped
2 cooked chicken breasts, boned and sliced thin
1/2 C heavy cream
salt and freshly ground pepper, to taste

Heat the vegetable oil in a heavy skillet and fry the tortillas on both sides - do not let them become crisp or brown.

Grease an ovenproof casserole. Mix together the enchilada sauce and the chopped jalapeños. Place a layer of the sauce in the bottom of the casserole. Follow with a layer of tortillas, then a layer of sliced chicken. Repeat this process until all ingredients are used up ending with a layer of tortillas.

Pour the cream over all and bake for 30 to 35 minutes at 350 until heated through. Serves 4.

Chicken and Cheese Celaya

 2 lb chicken breasts
2 C chicken stock
1 C water
5 cloves garlic, minced or pressed
1 bay leaf
3 green onions, thinly sliced
1/4 C cilantro, chopped
1/2 t oregano, crumbled
1/2 t salt
1/4 t pepper
2 T vegetable oil
2 T chile powder
3 T all purpose flour
1/8 t cumin
1/8 t cinnamon
1/3 C tomato sauce
1 doz corn tortillas (6-7 in), warmed
1/2 C sharp cheddar cheese
1/2 C Monterey Jack cheese

Arrange chicken breasts in heavy medium saucepan. Add stock, water, 2 cloves of garlic and bay leaf. Bring to boil. Reduce heat, cover and simmer until chicken is cooked through - about 12 minutes. Transfer chicken to bowl using slotted spoon and cool. Discard bay leaf and reserve poaching liquid. Peel skin off chicken and remove meat from bones. Tear meat into strips and place in a large bowl. Mix in green onions, cilantro, oregano, salt and pepper.

Heat 2 tablespoons oil in a heavy medium saucepan over medium-high heat. Add 3 minced garlic cloves and sauté 30 seconds. Add chile powder and sauté 1 minute longer. Add flour, cumin and cinnamon and stir 1 minute. Whisk in 1 cup reserved poaching liquid. Add remaining poaching liquid and tomato sauce. Cook until thick and smooth, whisking frequently - about 5 minutes. Cool slightly.

Lightly oil a 13 x 9 x 2 baking dish. Spoon 1/3 of the chicken mixture in the bottom of the prepared dish. Cover with 1/3 of the sauce and top with 4 of the warmed tortillas. Repeat the process ending with 4 tortillas. Sprinkle evenly with the 2 cheeses and cover with foil.

Preheat oven to 425 and bake, covered, for 15 minutes. Uncover and bake until hot and bubbling - about 10 minutes. Serves 6.

J.A.'s Chicken Casserole

1 doz corn tortilas, (6-7 in)
5 C chicken broth

1 lb mushrooms, thinly sliced
4 T butter
2 T vegetable oil

1 medium onion, thinly sliced
10 T butter
10 T flour
salt and freshly ground pepper, to taste

1 can (4 oz) diced green chiles
1 can (8 oz) chopped tomatoes, drained
4 to 6 C cooked chicken, boned and chopped
heavy cream, if needed
1 lb Monterey Jack cheese, shredded

Soften tortillas by dipping them briefly in hot chicken broth. Drain them and set aside.

Heat 4 tablespoons butter and 2 tablespoons vegetable oil and sauté the mushrooms until browned lightly. Remove and set aside.

In the same skillet heat the 10 tablespoons butter and sauté the onions until soft and translucent. Add flour and cook until lightly browned. Add chicken broth slowly, stirring constantly. Add the chiles, tomatoes, chicken and the sautéed mushrooms. Thin out with heavy cream, as necessary. Adjust seasonings with salt and pepper, to taste.

Butter an 11 x 9 x 2 inch baking dish. Line with 4 of the softened tortillas. Spoon about 1/3 of the chicken mixture over the tortillas followed by 1/3 the mushrooms. Sprinkle with cheese. Repeat process twice more, ending with cheese. Bake at 350 for 35 to 40 minutes. (May be refrigerated for up to 1 day but increase the baking time accordingly). Serves 8 to 10.

Ground Beef Enchilada Casserole with Ham and Cheese

1 1/2 lb ground beef (lean)
1 medium onion, chopped
1 pkg taco seasoning mix (1 1/4 oz)
1 C water
1/2 C prepared salsa
10 corn tortillas (6-7 inch)
2 pkg frozen chopped thawed spinach (10 oz each)
3 C Montery Jack cheese (grated)
1/2 lb cooked ham, diced
1 C sour cream

Combine ground beef and onion in a skillet. Brown over high heat, stirring meat to crumble. Stir in taco seasoning mix and water. Cover and simmer 10 minutes.

Pour half the salsa into a 3 quart baking pan or casserole. Coat 5 of the tortillas in the sauce to coat lightly and spread them, overlapping, in the bottom of the dish.

Press out most of the water from the spinach in a wire strainer; salt lightly. Stir half of it into the beef mixture. Spoon the mixture over the tortillas in casserole and sprinkle with half the cheese. Cover with remaining tortillas, overlapping, and spread the balance of the salsa over them. Distribute ham on top and spread with sour cream. Scatter the spinach over the cream - then top evenly with remaining cheese.

Cover and bake at 375 for 30 minutes. Uncover and continue baking for 15 minutes until heated through and bubbling around edges. Serves 8.

Turkey and Vegetables a la Mexicana

1 lb ground turkey
1 bunch green onions, thinly sliced
1 T chile powder
1 t garlic powder
1 lb zucchini, thinly sliced
1 pkg (10 oz) frozen corn, thawed
2 C enchilada sauce (divided)
1 can (3 oz) diced green chiles
1/4 t salt
8 corn tortillas (7-8 in)
1 can (16 oz) refried beans
1 C sharp cheddar cheese, grated
1/2 C sour cream (for garnish)

Cook the turkey, onions, chile powder and garlic powder in skillet over high heat, stirring often until turkey is no longer pink.

Add the zucchini, corn, 1 cup of the enchilada sauce, the green chiles and the salt. Cook over medium-high heat for about 10 minutes, stirring often, until zucchini is tender but still crisp. Remove from heat.

Grease a 9 x 13 x 2 baking dish. Layer with 4 tortillas on the bottom of the pan. (Tear them to fit if necessary). Spread refried beans evenly on top. Add the turkey mixture and another layer of tortillas. Pour remaining enchilada sauce over and sprinkle with cheese.

Bake at 350 for 30 minutes. Top each serving with a tablespoon of sour cream. Serves 8.

Quick Turkey Enchilada Casserole

2 C diced turkey, cooked
3 cans (10 oz each) enchilada sauce
2 C onions, minced
1 can (10 oz) cream of mushroom soup, condensed
1 can (16 oz) black pitted olives
6 corn tortillas (6 to 7 in)
2 C cheddar cheese, grated

Combine turkey, 2 cans of the sauce, onions, cream of mushroom soup and olives.

Cut the tortillas in strips. Use 1/2 to line the bottom of a greased 9 x 9 casserole (2 1/2 quart). Pour in 1/2 of the filling, cover with remaining tortilla strips and top with 1/2 of the cheese. Pour on rest of filling and top with remaining can of enchilada sauce and cheese.

Bake at 350 for 45 minutes. Serves 6.

Sour Cream Enchilada Casserole

1 onion, chopped
2 cloves garlic, minced or pressed
3 T vegetable oil
1 lb ground chuck
1 1/2 C bottled (or canned) green chile salsa
1 1/2 t dried oregano, crumbled
2 t chile powder
2 t ground cumin
salt and freshly ground pepper, to taste
2 C fresh (or frozen) corn kernels
1 T butter
1 small red bell pepper, thinly sliced
1 small green bell pepper, thinly sliced
6 corn tortillas (6-7 in)
2 C sour cream
2 C Montery Jack cheese, grated
1/2 C pitted black olives, sliced

In a skillet, cook the onion and garlic in 2 tablespoons oil over moderately-low heat. Stir often until they are softened. Add the chuck and cook the mixture over moderate heat. Stir and break up lumps until meat is no longer pink. Stir in the salsa and the spices. Add salt and pepper, to taste. Bring mixture to boil and simmer for 5 minutes.

In another skillet, cook the corn in the butter in the remaining 1 tablespoon oil over moderately-low heat, stirring for 3 minutes. Stir in the bell peppers (add salt and pepper, to taste) until peppers are softened, about 3 minutes.

Put 2 tortillas side by side, in an oval 2 quart casserole. Top them with one third the meat mixture, one third the sour cream and one third the cheese. Layer the remaining tortillas, meat mixture, sour cream and cheese in the same manner. Sprinkle the top layer of cheese with the olives. Spoon the corn mixture around the edge of the dish and bake at 375 for 30 minutes. Serves 6.

Tortilla Tamale Pie

2 lb beef chuck, diced
1 T vegetable oil
1 medium onion, chopped
2 cloves garlic, minced or pressed
3 jalapeño peppers, stemmed, seeded and chopped
1 1/2 t salt
1/2 t black pepper
1/4 t marjoram
1/4 t oregano
1 T flour
1 can (10 oz) red chile sauce
2 C water
1/2 C raisins
1/2 C sliced ripe olives, drained
8 corn tortillas (6-7 in)
vegetable oil for frying

Sauté beef in the 1 tablespoon oil. Add onion, garlic, jalapeño and seasonings. Stir in flour and gradually stir in chile sauce and water. Cover and simmer until meat is tender. Stir in raisins and olives.

In another pan, heat 1/2 inch vegetable oil. Dip each tortilla in hot oil, then in the hot chile mixture. In a 9 x 13 x 2 inch baking dish, overlap 5 tortillas, extending them up 2 inches on all sides of the dish. Fill with chile mixture (save out 1/2 cup liquid). Top with remaining 3 tortillas. Lap side and end tortillas over top. Moisten top with chile liquid. Cover and bake at 350 for 30 minutes. Makes 8 servings.

Ground Beef Bake Sonora

1 lb lean ground beef
1 can (17 oz) whole kernel corn, drained
1 C tomato sauce
1 C prepared salsa
1 T chile powder
1 1/2 t ground cumin
1 carton (16 oz) cottage cheese, low fat
2 eggs, slightly beaten
1/3 C Parmesan cheese, grated
1 t oregano leaves, crumbled
1/2 t garlic salt
1 doz corn tortillas, (6-7 in)
3/4 C sharp cheddar cheese, grated
3/4 C Monterey Jack cheese, grated

Brown meat until crumbly. Add corn, tomato sauce, salsa, chile powder and cumin. Simmer, stirring frequently for 5 minutes.

Combine cottage cheese, Parmesan cheese, oregano and garlic salt. Mix well.

Grease a 13 x 9 x 2 inch baking dish. Place one cup of the meat mixture evenly over the bottom of the dish. Cover with six of the tortillas, overlapping as necessary. Place one half of the remaining meat mixture over the tortillas and then one half of the cheese mixture. Cover with the remaining six tortillas followed by the remainder of the meat mixture and then the cheese mixture. Top with the cheddar cheese and bake at 375 for about 30 minutes or until hot and bubbly. Remove from oven and sprinkle with the Monterey Jack cheese. Let stand for 10 minutes before serving. Pass additional salsa. Serves 8.

Tortilla "Lasagna"

1 large onion, chopped
4 cloves garlic, minced or pressed
3 T olive oil
3 1/2 C canned tomatoes, undrained
1 can (15 oz) tomato purée
2 C beef broth
2 bay leaves
1/2 t salt
1/4 t coarse ground black pepper
1/8 t hot red pepper flakes
1/4 t oregano
1/4 t thyme
1 lb lean ground beef
1 doz flour tortillas, (9-10 in)
1 lb ricotta cheese
1 lb mozzarella cheese, sliced
1 C Parmesan cheese, grated

Sauté the onion and garlic in the olive oil until golden brown, stirring often. Add the tomatoes, tomato purée, beef broth, bay leaves, salt, pepper and red pepper flakes. Cover and simmer slowly for one hour. Uncover and simmer an additional 45 minutes. Stir in the oregano and thyme and simmer for 15 minutes longer. Add a little water if sauce becomes too thick. (Remove the bay leaves).

Sauté the ground beef in a skillet until meat is crumbly and no longer red. Season with a little salt and pepper.

Cut the tortillas in one inch strips. Grease a 13 x 9 x 2 inch baking dish and cover the bottom with one cup of the tomato sauce. Line the dish with 1/2 of the tortilla strips, 1/3 the remaining sauce, 1/2 the ground beef, 1/2 the mozzarella slices, 1/2 of the ricotta cheese (in slivers) and a little Parmesan cheese. Repeat the process with another layer of tortilla strips, ground beef, mozzarella and ricotta. Pour the remaining tomato sauce evenly over the top and sprinkle with the remaining Parmesan cheese.

Bake at 350 for 45 minutes or until the top is golden and bubbling. Cool for at least 10 minutes before serving. Serves 10-12.

Tortilla Crust Casserole

1 flour tortilla (9-10 inch)
6 oz pork sausage, bulk
1 clove garlic, minced or pressed
1 medium onion, diced
1 can (4 oz) diced green chiles
1/2 t ground cumin
3 eggs
1 cup sour cream
1 C sharp cheddar cheese, shredded
1/8 t cayenne pepper
1 ripe avocado, sliced (dip in lemon juice)

Press tortilla into 9 inch pie pan. Place in 375 oven to crisp evenly (about 5 minutes). Set aside.

In 10-12 inch skillet, stir sausage, onion and garlic over medium heat until meat is browned. Stir in chiles and cumin. Set aside.

In a bowl, beat eggs, 3/4 C sour cream, cheese and hot pepper seasoning. Stir in meat mixture and pour over tortilla shell. Bake until center jiggles slightly when gently shaken (about 30 minutes).

Lay avocado slices on top and spoon remaining sour cream in center. Cut into wedges. Serves 4.

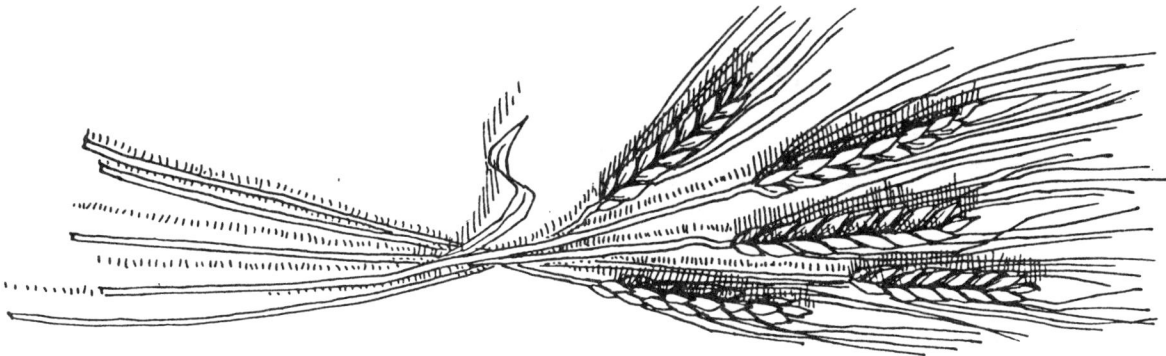

Roll 'Em Up Red Bean Casserole

1 large onion, chopped
4 cloves garlic, minced or pressed
3 T olive oil
2 cans (1 lb each) red beans, drained
1 C tomato sauce
2 t ground cumin
salt and freshly ground pepper, to taste
5 jalapeño chiles, seeded and chopped
1/3 C cilantro, chopped
1 doz flour tortillas (8-9 inch), warmed
2 C Monterey Jack cheese, grated
guacamole and salsa fresca (or prespared salsa)

Cook the onion and the garlic in a heavy skillet over moderately low heat. Stir often until onion is softened. Add the beans and mash them partially with the back of a wooden spoon. Add the tomato sauce, the jalapeños and the spices. Simmer, stirring, for 5 minutes - or until slightly thickened. Stir in the cilantro and remove from heat.

Spread about 3 tablespoons of the mixture down the center of a warmed tortilla and roll it up enclosing the filling but keeping the ends open. Arrange, seam side down in a large baking dish. Repeat the process with the remaining tortillas, placing them in the baking dish in a single layer.

Sprinkle the rolled up tortillas with the cheese and bake the casserole, covered with foil, at 350 for 15 minutes. Serve with guacamole and your favorite salsa. Serves 6.

Curried Turkey Royale

8 corn tortillas, (5-7 in)
1 small onion, chopped
1 small green bell pepper, chopped
2 cloves garlic, minced or pressed
2 T butter or margarine
2 C cooked turkey, chopped
1 can (16 oz) tomatoes, cut up
1/4 C dried currants
2 T parsley, chopped
2 T curry powder, or to taste
1 t salt
1/8 t freshly ground pepper
dash ground mace
2 T sherry
1 T cornstarch
3/4 C Monterey Jack cheese, grated

In a saucepan cook onion, bell pepper and garlic in butter until tender but not brown.

Stir in turkey, undrained tomatoes, currants, parsley, curry powder, salt, pepper and mace. Cook, stirring occasionally, until heated through - about 10 minutes. Blend the sherry into the cornstarch and stir it into the turkey mixture. Cook, stirring constantly, until mixture is thickened and bubbly.

Arrange 2 tortillas in a greased 13 x 9 x 2 inch baking dish. Spread 1/3 the sauce over them and sprinkle with 1/3 the cheese. Repeat the process twice with tortillas, sauce and then cheese.

Bake, uncovered, at 350 until heated through - about 25 minutes. Makes 4 servings.

Eggplant "Lasagne"

2 lb eggplant
2 cans peeled chopped tomatoes (14 1/2 oz each)
2 lb fresh Italian plum tomatoes, peeled and sliced
6 T olive oil
1 large onion, chopped
3 cloves garlic, minced or pressed
1 t salt
1/4 t pepper
1 t basil, crumbled
1/2 t thyme, crumbled
1/8 t red pepper flakes
1/2 C dry vermouth
8 flour tortillas, (9-10 in)
1 lb ricotta cheese
1/2 C Parmesan cheese, grated
1 lb mozzarella cheese, sliced

Peel the eggplant and slice it 1/2 inch thick, lengthwise. Salt the slices on both sides and let them drain in a colander for about 45 minutes. Rinse them off. Squeeze out the excess moisture and dice them into 1/2 inch pieces. Sauté the eggplant in 3 tablespoons olive oil over high heat, stirring or tossing them constantly until tender.

Heat remaining 3 tablespoons of the olive oil in a large saucepan and sauté the onions and garlic until they become soft and transparent. Add the cannned tomatoes, the sliced Italian tomatoes, salt, pepper, basil, thyme, red pepper flakes and the vermouth. Cover and simmer, stirring occasionally, for 15 minutes. Uncover and simmer an additional 15 minutes, stirring occasionally. Sauce will still be juicy, but somewhat thickened.

Slice the tortillas in one inch strips. Grease an 9 x 13 x 2 inch baking pan. Spoon 1/3 of the tomato sauce across the bottom and arrange 1/3 of the tortilla strips over it. Spread on 1/2 the ricotta cheese and sprinkle with several tablespoons of the Parmesan cheese. Evenly distribute 1/2 the cooked eggplant over the cheeses. Cover with 1/3 the sliced mozzarella and spoon on another 1/3 the sauce. Make another layer of tortilla strips and cover with the rest of the ricotta. Sprinkle on some more Parmesan cheese and cover with the remaining eggplant. Arrange another 1/3 of the mozzarella slices over the eggplant. Make a third layer of tortilla strips. Cover with the remaining mozzarella, spoon over the remaining sauce and sprinkle on the rest of the Parmesan cheese.

Cover with aluminum foil and bake at 350 for 30 minutes. Place under the broiler for 5 to 10 minutes or until the cheese is browned. Serves 8-10.

Western Black Bean and Beef Bake

1 C dried black beans
1 can (7 3/4 oz) Mexican style tomato sauce
1 can (7 3/4 oz) tomato sauce
1/2 C beef broth
1 lb lean ground beef
1/2 t dehydrated onion
1/4 t dried oregano
1/2 t garlic salt
6 flour tortillas (9-10 in)
3/4 lb Monterey Jack cheese with jalapeño peppers, grated

Cook beans according to package directions. Drain and reserve.

Mix together the tomato sauces and the broth. Set aside.

Sauté the ground beef in a little olive oil. Mix in the onion, oregano and the garlic salt. Stir mixture until juices evaporate and beef is well browned. Remove skillet from heat.

Lightly grease a 13 x 9 x 2 inch baking dish. Cover the bottom of the dish with one cup of the tomato mixture. Overlap 3 of the tortillas over the sauce. Place the cooked beans evenly over the tortillas followed by all the ground beef mixture. Cover with 1/2 the grated cheese. Overlap the remaining 3 tortillas over the mixture and then pour the tomato sauce over the tortillas. Cover with the remaining grated cheese and bake at 350 for 20 to 25 minutes or until top is golden and bubbly. Serves 8.

Spinach-Mushroom Pirámide

1 large onion, finely chopped
3/4 lb mushrooms, thinly sliced
2 slices bacon, finely chopped
3 large cloves garlic, minced or pressed
1 t dry tarragon leaves
2 pkg (10 oz each) frozen chopped spinach
   (thawed and moisture partially squeezed out)
1 C ricotta cheese
2 large eggs, slightly beaten
1/2 C parmesan cheese, grated
1/3 C cilantro, finely chopped
3 flour tortillas, (8-9 inch)
6 T prepared salsa

In a 12 inch frying pan over medium heat, stir onion, mushrooms, bacon, garlic and tarragon often until liquid evaporates and onion is golden brown - about 20 minutes. Remove pan from heat.

Mix ricotta with beaten eggs and add crumbled spinach, parmesan cheese and cilantro. Add it to the mushroom mixture and mix well.

Grease well a 3 quart casserole. Moisten the tortillas slightly by holding them under running water for a few seconds. Place one tortilla at the bottom of the casserole. Place 1/3 the spinach- mushroom mixture over the tortilla, then place 1/3 the mushroom mixture. Repeat the layers. Spoon 4 tablespoons prepared salsa over the top. Bake at 350 for 35 to 40 minutes or until filling is set. Let rest for 10 minutes and unmold onto a serving dish. Place 2 tablespoons salsa on top. Cut into wedges and serve offering more salsa, as desired. Makes 6 servings.

Tortilla "Manicotti"

3/4 lb lean ground beef
1 small onion, chopped
2 cloves garlic, minced or pressed
1 can (8 oz) tomato sauce
1 can (7 oz) tomato paste
1 1/2 t dried basil, crushed
1/2 t sugar
1/2 t fennel seed, crushed
1 C beef broth
1/2 t salt
2 eggs, beaten
3 C ricotta
1/2 C Parmesan cheese, grated
2 T fresh parsley, minced
8 flour tortillas, (9-10 in)
1 lb mozzarella cheese, shredded

Brown ground beef with onion and garlic. Drain. Add tomato sauce, tomato paste, basil, sugar fennel, beef broth and salt. Simmer, covered, for 15 minutes, stirring often.

Mix eggs, ricotta, Parmesan, parsley and a little salt and pepper, to taste.

Cut tortillas in half. Place half of them, overlapping, in the bottom of a greased 13 x 9 x 2 inch baking dish. Arrange the egg filling evenly over the tortillas and then place the remaining tortillas on top. Spoon the sauce over the tortillas.

Cover and bake at 350 for 30 minutes. Uncover and sprinkle with the mozzarella. Return to oven and bake until cheese melts - about 10 minutes. Makes 8 servings.

Tortilla Bake Florentine

1 lb bulk Italian sausage, mild
1 jar (15 1/2 oz) spaghetti sauce with mushrooms
   (or 2 C of your favorite sauce)
6 flour tortillas (9-10 in)
2 C cottage cheese, cream-style
1 pkg (10 oz) frozen chopped spinach, cooked and well drained
1/2 C Parmesan cheese, grated
      cilantro sprigs, optional

In a skillet slowly brown the sausage. Pour off excess fat and add spaghetti sauce. Simmer, uncovered, for 10 minutes.

Hold the tortillas for a few seconds under running water. Shake off the excess water and arrange 3 tortillas in a greased 12 x 9 x 2 inch baking dish. Overlap the edges so that bottom of dish is well covered.

Spread half the cottage cheese and half the sauce evenly over the tortillas. Evenly cover with all the drained spinach. Repeat layering with remaining 3 tortillas, cottage cheese and sauce.

Sprinkle with the Parmesan cheese, cover. Bake at 375 for 45 minutes. Let stand 10 minutes before serving. Garnish with sprigs of cilantro. Makes 6 servings.

Acapulco Casserole

1 C chopped onion
1 C chopped celery
2 T butter or margarine
2 cans (15 oz each) chile with beans
2 cans (15 oz ea) refried beans
1 can (12 oz) whole kernel corn, drained
2 cans (4 oz ea) taco sauce
1/4 t salt
10 corn tortillas (7-8 in), cut in 1 inch strips
1 C (4 oz) sharp cheddar cheese, grated
    fresh cilantro sprigs for garnish

In saucepan, cook onion and celery in butter or margarine until tender but not brown, about 10 minutes.

Stir in chile, refried beans, corn, taco sauce, and salt. Arrange half the tortilla strips in 13 x 9 x 2 inch baking dish; top with half the chile mixture. Repeat layers.

Bake, covered, in 350 oven for 45 to 50 minutes. Sprinkle cheese on top. Bake, uncovered, last 10 minutes to melt cheese. Garnish with sprigs of fresh cilantro, if desired. Makes 8 servings.

Traditional Enchiladas and *Nouveau* Enchiladas

Enchiladas Coloradas

    1 1/2 lb sharp cheddar cheese, grated
    5 medium onions, finely chopped
    3 T olive oil
    2 1/2 C salsa colorada (recipe follows)
    10 flour tortillas, (9-10 in)
    1 can pitted black olives

Sauté onions in the olive oil for about 20 minutes until very soft, but not browned. (Prepare salsa coloradas while onions are cooking).

Grease 2 baking pans. Dip each tortilla in the warm salsa roja and place them on a plate. Put 1/4 cup grated cheese, 2 tablespoons onion and 2 olives down the center of each tortilla. Fold over the sides and gently transfer, folded edges down, to a baking pan. Sprinkle a few tablespoon of sauce over the enchiladas and garnish with cheese and olives.

Bake at 350 for 20 minutes. Pass remaining sauce at the table. Serves 8.

Salsa Colorada

    12 ancho chiles
    4 C water
    1/2 C chopped onion
    4 garlic cloves, unpeeled
    1 1/2 C tomatoes, chopped, unpeeled
    1/2 t salt

Toast chiles on a baking sheet in 250 oven for 10 minutes. Rinse with cold water. Remove stems. In covered pot, simmer the chiles, tomatoes, onions, garlic and salt in the water for 1/2 hour. Push chiles down into the liquid every 5 minutes as they simmer. Purée in a food processor or blender (water and all) in several batches. Push through wire strainer to remove skins and seeds. Simmer sauce for 10 minutes.

Enchiladas with Salsa Verde

2 lb tomatillos (or 24 oz canned tomatillos)
5 small jalapeño peppers, seeded and minced
1/2 C fresh cilantro, chopped
1 t salt
1 medium onion, finely chopped
vegetable oil
1 1/2 lb fresh mozzarella cheese, cut in thin strips
16 corn tortillas (6-7 in)
1/2 lb feta cheese, crumbled
cilantro sprigs for garnish, optional
prepared salsa

To make salsa verde, peel the dry skin off tomatillos and wash. Boil tomatillos in lightly salted water for 10 minutes, or until they are just soft. Drain and purée them in a blender or processor. Put them in a saucepan with the minced jalapeño peppers, half of the chopped cilantro, the salt, and half of the chopped onion. Simmer the sauce for about 1/2 hour.

Heat a little vegetable oil in a skillet and fry a tortilla in it for about 20 seconds per side. Put several strips of the mozzarella cheese on it, spread about 1 teaspoon of the salsa verde over the cheese and sprinkle 1 teaspoon of the remaining onions over the sauce. Roll the tortilla around the filling. Place the tortilla, seam side down in a lightly oiled baking dish. Repeat the process until all the tortillas are used up. Place tortillas close together in pan. (Use a little more oil in skillet as you fry the tortillas.)

Bake at 350 for 20 to 25 minutes. Sprinkle feta cheese and the remaining cilantro over them and serve immediately. Garnish platter or individual serving dishes with sprigs of cilantro. Pass   salsa separately. Makes 6 to 8 servings.

Shredded Beef Enchiladas

vegetable oil
1 medium onion, chopped
2 cans (7 oz each) diced green chiles
1/2 t ground cumin
1 T all-purpose flour
2 C sour cream
3/4 lb Monterey Jack cheese, shredded
1 doz corn tortillas (6-7 in)
    shredded beef (recipe follows)

In an 8-10 inch skillet, combine 2 tablespoons oil, the onion, chiles and cumin. Cook, stirring occasionally, over medium heat until onion is soft - about 15 minutes.

Mix in the flour, then blend in 1 cup sour cream and stir until simmering. Remove from heat and blend in 1 cup cheese. Salt to taste.

Pour 1/2 inch oil into a 7-8 inch skillet. Set over medium-high heat until hot. Cook tortillas, 1 at a time, until surface bubbles and tortillas are still limp - about 5 seconds on each side. Lay the tortillas flat on paper towels to drain.

Spoon about 1/3 cup chile mixture and 1/4 cup shredded beef down center of each tortilla. Roll to enclose and set them, seam side down, in a shallow 12 x 15 inch baking pan or dish. (If made ahead, cover and chill as long as overnight).

Bake, uncovered, at 350 until hot in center - about 20 minutes (about 25 minutes if chilled). Sprinkle remaining cheese evenly on top and return to oven until cheese melts - about 5 minutes more.

Use a wide spatula to transfer enchiladas to dinner plates. Offer remaining sour cream to spoon on top. Serves 6.

Shredded Beef

Place a 3 pound boneless beef chuck roast in a 5 to 6 quart pan. Cover with water and simmer for 2 to 2 1/2 hours. Remove the meat and shred. (Reserve stock). Brown the shredded meat and add 2 tablespoons chile powder and 1 teaspoon ground cumin. Add 1 cup reserved stock and simmer for 30 minutes - do not allow to dry - adding more stock, as needed.

Enchiladas de Guajolote Teotihuacán

1 lb cooked turkey, shredded (about 2 cups)
2 C prepared green chile salsa
1/2 lb (2 cups) sharp cheddar cheese, grated
8 oz plain yogurt
2 T fresh cilantro, chopped
1/2 t ground cumin
1/4 t crushed dried hot red chiles
6 flour tortillas (7-8 in)
6 large pitted ripe olives

In a large bowl, combine turkey, 1 cup of the salsa, 1 cup cheese, yogurt, cilantro, cumin and dried chiles.

Place tortillas on a flat surface. Top evenly with turkey mixture. Roll up and place, seam down in a greased 8 x 12 x 2 inch baking pan. Evenly top with the remaining salsa and cheese.

Bake, uncovered at 350 until cheese is bubbly and enchiladas are hot in the center - about 20 minutes. Top each enchilada with an olive. Makes 6 servings.

Enchiladas Oaxaqueñas

6 dried ancho chiles
6 dried pasilla chiles
6 dried Anaheim chiles
boiling water
3 large Roma tomatoes
6 garlic cloves, cut in halves
1 medium onion, sliced
2 T corn oil
1 cinnamon stick
   chicken broth (if necessary)
2/3 Mexican chocolate round (3.3 oz size)
2 t sugar
1/2 t dried oregano, crumbled
    salt and freshly ground pepper
    corn oil for frying
1 1/2 doz corn tortillas (6-7 in)
1/2 lb queso fresco or feta cheese, crumbled
1 large onion, minced
1/4 C fresh parsley, minced

Place all chiles in large heavy pot over medium heat until slightly darkened and fragrant. Turn occasionally - about 4 minutes. Pour boiling water over them, to cover, and soak until softened about 15 minutes. Drain chiles. Remove stems (and seeds, if desired). Reserve liquid.

Transfer chiles to blender. In the same pot, cook tomatoes, garlic and onion over medium heat until tomatoes are lightly charred and garlic and onion are browned. Turn frequently - about 15 minutes. Add to chiles and purée until smooth. (Add enough of the reserved soaking mixture to moisten, if necessary).

Melt 2 tablespoons of oil in the same pot over low heat. Add chile mixture and cinnamon and simmer until thickened. Stir frequently to prevent burning - about 10 minutes. (Use chicken broth to thin, if necessary). Mix in chocolate, sugar, oregano and salt and pepper, to taste. Simmer 5 minutes to blend flavors and melt chocolate, stirring frequently. Remove cinnamon stick. Cover and keep sauce warm.

Heat 1/4 inch oil in a heavy large skillet over medium heat. Add 1 tortilla and cook 30 seconds. Turn and cook second side 15 seconds. Add to sauce, carefully folding into half and then into quarter until heated through. Transfer tortilla to serving plate. Repeat with remaining tortillas. Spoon additional sauce over. Garnish with cheese, minced onion and fresh parsley. Serve at once. Makes 8 servings.

Chicken Enchiladas Verdes

5 chiles poblanos
1 lb tomatillos
1 C sour cream
2 eggs, beaten
1 t salt
1 t pepper
1/4 C cilantro leaves, chopped
1 small onion, chopped
12 corn tortillas (7-8 in)
    vegetable oil (for frying tortillas)
2 C cooked chicken, shredded
1 1/2 C Monterey Jack cheese, shredded

Toast the chiles on a hot griddle over medium heat, turning frequently, until the skin blisters - or hold over a gas burner until charred. Place chiles in a tightly closed plastic bag for about 15 minutes to allow them to steam.

Remove and discard stems. Cut chiles lengthwise in half and discard seeds. Peel the outer brown covering from the tomatillos and place in a saucepan. Add water to cover and cook over low heat until tomatoes are light green - about 15 minutes. Drain.

Place chiles, tomatillos, sour cream, eggs, salt and pepper in a blender or food processor and blend until smooth. Place in a sauce pan and add the chopped cilantro and onion. Heat the mixture over low heat, stirring occasionally - about 5 minutes.

Fry the tortillas, one at a time, in hot vegetable oil until soft - about 1/2 minute per side. Dip the tortillas, 1 at a time, into the sauce. On a work surface, place about 3 tablespoons shredded chicken on each tortilla. Fold in half and place in baking dish. Repeat process using as many baking dishes as necessary. Bake, covered at 350 for 20 minutes. Makes 6 servings.

Creamy Chicken Enchiladas

2 T butter
1 medium onion, thinly sliced
1 C cooked chicken, shredded
1/2 C canned green chiles, diced
4 oz cream cheese, diced
    salt
1/4 C vegetable oil
4 corn tortillas (6-7 in)
1/3 C whipping cream
1 C Monterey Jack cheese, grated
    prepared salsa

Melt butter in heavy large skillet over low heat. Add onion and sauté until limp but not brown - about 10 minutes. Remove from heat. Mix in chicken, chiles and cream cheese. Season with salt, to taste.

Heat oil in heavy small skillet over medium heat. Add tortillas one at a time and fry until just beginning to blister, turning once - about one minute. Drain on paper towels.

Spoon 1/2 cup chicken filling down center of each tortilla and roll. Place enchiladas, seam side down, in a glass baking dish. Pour cream over. Sprinkle with cheese and bake at 350 until cream thickens and cheese bubbles - about 20 minutes. Serve hot with salsa. Makes 2 servings.

Enchiladas Suizas with Spinach

2 lb fresh spinach
3 T vegetable oil
2 T butter
1 medium onion, chopped
3 cloves garlic, minced or pressed
   salt and freshly ground pepper, to taste
1 lb Swiss cheese, grated
1 doz corn tortillas (6-7 in)
   vegetable oil
1 T flour
1 C milk, heated
1 C sour cream (room temperature)
1/2 C diced green chiles
1/8 t red pepper flakes
   sour cream and cilantro sprigs for garnish (optional)

Wash spinach leaves carefully, remove stems, drain and then chop them. Heat the oil and 1 tablespoon butter in a large skillet. Sauté the onions and garlic until soft and golden. Add spinach and toss in hot oil until wilted. Salt and pepper, to taste, and continue cooking over medium heat until all liquid is absorbed, stirring often.

Take a tortilla, brush lightly with oil and heat it quickly in a skillet on both sides until soft and flexible. Spread a tablespoon of grated cheese down the center of tortilla - then spread with a tablespoon of the spinach. Fold one end of the tortilla over the filling and roll it up. Repeat with remaining tortillas.

Lightly oil a large shallow pan and arrange the enchiladas, seam side down. Make a sauce by melting the remaining 1 tablespoon butter in a pan and stirring in the flour. Cook over low heat, stirring constantly, until it is golden. Add the heated milk and using a whisk stir it until slightly thickened. Add sour cream, diced chiles, red pepper flakes and remaining cheese. Cook over low heat until the cheese is melted and sauce is smooth. Season with salt and pepper, to taste. Pour sauce over the enchiladas. Cover with foil and bake at 350 for about 25 minutes.

Place under a broiler for a few minutes to brown the top. Garnish with sour cream and cilantro sprigs. Makes 6 servings.

Breakfast Enchiladas

1/2 C pepitas (pumpkin seeds) or sunflower seeds
2/3 C chicken broth
4 T lemon juice
3 cloves garlic, minced or pressed
2/3 C diced green chiles
    salt and freshly ground pepper, to taste
1 C whipping cream
10 large eggs
2 T milk
3 T butter
1/2 C chopped fresh cilantro
1/2 t dried red chile peppers, crushed
2/3 C green onions, chopped
1 doz corn tortillas (6-7 in)
    vegetable oil

Put the seeds, chicken broth, lemon juice, garlic and chiles in a blender or processor and whirl at high speed until mixture is well puréed. Add salt and pepper (to taste) and cream. Blend until mixed.

Beat eggs in a large bowl with the milk, salt and pepper (to taste) and the chopped cilantro. Melt butter in a large skillet. Heat the crushed red chiles for 1 minute and then add eggs. Stir constantly until they are set but still moist.

Heat a tortilla on a hot skillet that has been brushed with a little oil for 30 seconds to 1 minute on each side. (Tortilla should be very flexible). Spread 2 or 3 tablespoons of the cooked eggs down center of tortilla - then pour about 1 tablespoon of the sauce over the eggs. Roll up the tortilla over the filling. Repeat until egg mixture is used up.

Arrange enchiladas, seam side down, in an oiled baking dish and spoon the remainder of the sauce over them. Bake at 350 for about 25 minutes.

Place under broiler for a few moments to brown the top. Sprinkle enchiladas with the chopped green onions. Makes 6 servings.

Spinach-Raisin Enchiladas

1/4 C butter (1/2 stick)
2 T raisins
2 medium onions, chopped
3 pkg (10 oz ea) frozen chopped spinach, thawed
1/2 lb feta cheese (about 1/2 C)
1 can (10 oz) red enchilada sauce

2 T all-purpose flour
1 t ground nutmeg
1 t black pepper
3 C chicken broth (regular strength)
8 corn tortillas (6-7 in)

In a large skillet over medium heat, melt 1 tablespoon butter. Add raisins and stir until puffed - about 2 minutes. Remove from pan and set aside.

Add another 1 tablespoon butter to pan and melt. Add onions, stirring often over medium-high heat until limp - about 5 minutes.

Put spinach in a colander and squeeze as much liquid as possible from it. Mix spinach and onions in a bowl. Set aside 1 1/4 cups of the mixture. To remainder in bowl, add raisins and 1/4 cup of the cheese and mix together.

In the skillet, melt 2 more tablespoons butter over medium heat. Stir in the flour, nutmeg and pepper until well blended. Remove from heat and blend in 1 1/2 cups chicken broth until smooth. Bring to a boil, stirring, over high heat. Remove from heat and add 1/2 cup of the liquid to the spinach mixture in the bowl.

Combine remaining liquid, reserved 1 1/4 cups chicken broth and 1/2 cup of the cheese in a blender. Cover and whirl until sauce is smoothly puréed - about 3 to 5 minutes.

Pour about 1/4 inch vegetable oil into an 8 to 10 inch skillet. Set pan on medium-high heat. When oil is hot, add 1 tortilla at a time and cook just until softened - 2 to 4 second per side, turning once with tongs. Drain in a single layer on paper towels.

To assemble, place about 1/3 cup of the spinach-raisin filling down the center of a tortilla. Roll to enclose filling then place seam side down in a 9 x 13 x 2 inch baking dish. Repeat process, placing them side by side in the dish.

Pour puréed spinach sauce over tortillas, spreading to coat them completely and evenly. Bake, uncovered, at 350 for about 25 minutes or until heated through. While enchiladas are baking, warm the enchilada sauce over direct heat. Sprinkle enchiladas with the remaining cheese. Drizzle a little sauce over all. Offer remaining sauce to spoon onto individual portions. Makes 8 enchiladas.

Tex-Mex Enchiladas with Ham and Sour Cream

1 C chopped ham
1/2 lb Monterey Jack cheese, grated
1/2 C diced green chiles
1/2 C sour cream
1/2 C chopped fresh cilantro
8 flour tortillas (6-7 in)
1/2 C butter
1/2 C flour
4 C milk
1 lb sharp cheddar cheese, diced
2 t Dijon mustard
1 t salt
1 small onion, grated

In a bowl, combine the ham, cheese, chiles, sour cream and cilantro and mix well. Set aside.

In a medium saucepan over low heat, melt the butter and add the flour, stirring constantly, for 3-5 minutes. Gradually add the milk and cook, stirring, until the sauce is smooth and thick. Add the cheese and stir until the cheese is melted. Stir in the mustard, salt and onions. (Sauce may be made ahead and refrigerated - reheat before assembling).

To assemble, preheat oven to 350. Place 1/8 of the ham mixture near the edge of each tortilla and roll tightly. Place, seam side down, in an oiled baking dish. Repeat process with remaining 7 tortillas. Pour the sauce over the enchiladas covering them thoroughly. Bake for 20-25 minutes. Makes 8 enchiladas.

Turkey-Asparagus Enchiladas Divan

1 can (10 1/2) oz) cream of chicken soup, condensed
1 t Worcestershire sauce
    dash ground nutmeg
1 pkg (8 oz) frozen cut asparagus
2 C cooked turkey, chopped
6 flour tortillas (5-6in)
3/4 C Parmesan cheese, grated
1/2 C whipping cream
1/2 C mayonnaise

Blend together the soup, Worcestershire sauce and nutmeg. Set aside.

Cook asparagus according to package directions and drain.

Combine the asparagus and turkey. Blend in 1/4 cup of the sauce.

On a work surface, spoon about 1/2 cup filling along the center of each tortilla. Fold two sides towards the middle and place, seam side down,in a greased 13 x 9 x 2 inch baking dish. Spoon remaining sauce over the tortillas and top with half the cheese. Bake, covered, at 350 until heated through - about 25 minutes.

Whip cream until soft peaks form. Fold in the mayonnaise. Spread over the enchiladas. Top with remaining cheese and broil 3 to 4 inches from heat, until golden - about 3 minutes. Makes 6 enchiladas.

Chicken Enchiladas with Rum Sauce

4 whole medium chicken breasts, skinned, boned, halved lengthwise and cut in strips
2 T vegetable oil
1 medium onion, chopped
2 cloves garlic, minced or pressed
1 can (16 oz) tomatoes, cut up
2 T fresh lime juice
1 t salt
1/2 t dried oregano, crushed
1/8 t freshly ground pepper
1/4 C raisins
1 can (8 1/4 oz) pineapple chunks
1/3 C rum
2 T all-purpose flour
1/4 C cold water
6 flour tortillas, (9-10 in)

In a large skillet brown the chicken strips lightly in the oil. Add onion and garlic and cook until onion is tender.

Drain tomatoes - reserve the liquid. Set tomatoes aside. Add the reserved liquid, lime juice, salt, oregano and pepper to the chicken. Cover and simmer for 10 minutes. Add tomatoes and raisins. Simmer, covered for 5 minutes. Remove chicken and set aside.

Cut pineapple into smaller pieces and add to the sauce along with the rum. Blend water into flour and stir into sauce. Cook and stir until thickened and bubbly.

On a work surface, divide the chicken mixture evenly on the 6 tortillas. Fold the two opposite edges so they overlap the filling and place, seam side down, in a 13 x 9 x 2 inch baking dish. Spoon the sauce over the enchiladas, and bake at 350 for 25 minutes. Makes 6 enchiladas.

Chinese Enchiladas with Sweet and Sour Sauce

1/2 lb boneless pork, finely chopped
1 clove garlic, minced or pressed
1 T vegetable oil
2 C bok choy, finely shredded
1 C mushrooms, chopped
1/2 C onion, finely chopped
1/2 C celery, finely chopped
1/2 C water chestnuts, chopped
1/4 C carrot, shredded
1 can (4 1/2 oz) shrimp, drained and chopped
1 egg, beaten
2 T soy sauce
1 T sherry
1/2 t sugar
1 doz flour tortillas (9-10 in)
    Sweet and Sour Sauce (Recipe follows)

In skillet cook pork and garlic quickly in hot oil, stirring until meat is browned. Drain off fat. Add vegetables; cook and stir 2 to 3 minutes more. In bowl combine pork mixture with shrimp, egg, soy, sugar and 1/4 teaspoon salt. Cool.

Spoon equal amounts of filling in center of each tortilla. Fold in opposite ends and place, seam side down, in a greased 15 x 10 x 1 inch baking pan. Bake, uncovered at 350 for 20 minutes. Serve with Sweet and Sour Sauce. Makes 12 enchiladas.

Sweet and Sour Sauce:

In saucepan combine 1/2 cup packed brown sugar and 1 tablespoon cornstarch. Stir in 1/3 cup red wine vinegar, 1/3 cup chicken broth, 1/4 cup finely chopped green bell pepper, 2 tablespoons chopped pimento, 1 tablespoon soy sauce, 1/4 teaspoon garlic powder and 1/4 teaspoon ground ginger. Cook and stir until bubbly. Serve hot. Makes 1 1/4 cup sauce.

Microwave Enchiladas

3 T vegetable oil
2 cloves garlic, minced or pressed
3 T all-purpose flour
1 1/2 C water
1 can (10 oz) enchilada sauce
l t chile powder
3/4 t salt
1 1/2 lb lean ground beef
2 C sharp cheddar cheese, shredded
1/2 C black olives, sliced
1 T instant onion soup mix
1/2 t salt
1/4 t black pepper
1 doz corn tortillas (6-7 in)

Combine oil and garlic in 2 quart glass casserole. Cook on High for 2 minutes. Whisk in flour until smooth. Blend in water, sauce, chile powder and 3/4 teaspoon salt. Cook on High for 8 minutes stir several times while cooking. Set aside.

Crumble meat into another 2-quart glass casserole. Cook on High until no longer pink - stir occasionally for 5 to 6 minutes. Pour off fat. Blend in 1 cup cheese, olives, instant onion soup, salt and pepper.

Lightly butter 9 x 13 x 2 inch glass baking dish. Heat tortillas in package on High for 1 minute. Dip one tortilla in sauce. Spoon 1 heaping tablespoon meat mixture down center and roll up. Place in buttered dish, seam side down. Repeat process with remaining tortillas. Top with remaining sauce and cheese. Cook on High for 10 minutes and serve immediately. Makes 12 enchiladas.

Classic Tacos,
New Wave Tacos
and
Fajitas

Tacos de Carne Guisada
(Braised Beef Tacos)

2 lb chuck roast
2 T oil or lard
1 medium onion, sliced
2 cloves garlic, minced or pressed
1 C chicken broth, beef broth or water
1 bay leaf
1 t thyme
1/2 t oregano
1 T minced parsley
1 jalapeño pepper, seeds removed, finely minced
1 avocado, peeled and cubed, marinated in
1/4 C lime juice
16 flour tortillas
2 tomatoes, chopped
1/2 C shredded lettuce

Trim the meat. Heat the oil over high heat and brown the meat well. Reduce heat and add the onion, garlic, broth, bay leaf, thyme, oregano and parsley. Cover well and simmer together for an hour or until meat is fork tender.

Remove the meat and let cool. Shred into small pieces and keep warm.

Reduce the cooking liquid over high heat until only one quarter cup remains. Return the meat to this liquid and add the parsley and jalapeño. Keep warm.

Divide meat among the tortillas and add avocado, tomato, lettuce and salsa. Fold over and eat immediately. Makes 16 tacos.

Tacos de Huachinango

2 lb huachinango filets (red snapper)
1 C unbleached flour
2 eggs, separated
1/2 t garlic salt
1 t oregano
1/2 t black pepper
1/4 t cayenne pepper
3/4 C beer, room temperature
2 C vegetable oil
1 1/2 doz corn tortillas (7-8 in)
   salsa fresca or prepared salsa
2 C shredded cabbage
   prepared green taco sauce

Cut fish into strips about 2 inches wide and 3 inches long. Roll in flour and dust off excess. Set aside while mixing batter.

Beat egg yolks together with seasonings, beer and 3/4 cup flour until well blended.

Whisk the egg whites until they resemble soft whipped cream and then fold gently into batter. Set aside. (Batter holds for up to one hour).

Heat oil in large cast-iron skillet. Dip floured fish pieces in batter and carefully slip into hot oil. Fry until fish turns a deep gold turning so it browns evenly. Remove to paper towels to drain.

Warm corn tortillas on a griddle.

To assemble tacos, spread a heaping teaspoon of salsa over a warm tortilla. Add a heaping tablespoon of shredded cabbage. Add several pieces of fried fish and drizzle with taco sauce. Fold over and eat immediately. (Best to let guests assemble their own tacos at the table!) Makes 6 servings.

Tacos de Frijoles y Papas
(Bean and Potato Tacos)

3 small new potatoes (about 1 lb)
1 small onion, chopped
3 T butter
   salt and freshly ground pepper
1 doz corn tortillas (6-7 in)
   vegetable oil for frying tortillas
1 1/2 C refried beans
   prepared salsa or salsa fresca
   chopped cabbage and tomatoes, for garnish

Cut potatoes into cubes and boil them in salted water until almost tender. Drain.

In a skillet, sauté the chopped onion in the butter for a few minutes. Add the potatoes and saute this mixture, stirring often, until the potatoes are tender and slightly golden - about 10 minutes. Season to taste with salt and pepper.

Warm the tortillas quickly, one at a time, on a hot griddle. Do not allow them to become crisp, they should be soft and flexible.

Heat the refried beans and put one tablespoon on a tortilla, spreading it across in a thick line down the center - almost to the ends. Add a heaping tablespoon of the potatoes and arrange them over the beans. Fold the tortilla in half over the filling. Repeat process until all the tortillas are filled.

Right before serving, fry the tacos in a small amount of oil until they are crisp on both sides. Garnish with chopped cabbage and tomatoes and serve hot. Pass the salsa. Makes 6 servings.

Flautas

3 large ripe avocados
    juice of 1 large lemon
    salt, to taste
1 clove garlic, minced or pressed
1 large onion, minced
1 doz corn tortillas (6-7 in)
    vegetable oil for frying tortillas
1 C sour cream
1/2 lb feta cheese, crumbled
    prepared salsa

Peel and mash the avocado, stir in the lemon juice, salt, garlic and 1/2 cup of the minced onion.

Heat a tortilla on both sides over a gas flame (or in a lightly greased skillet). As soon as it is warm enough to roll without cracking, spread a heaping tablespoon of the avocado filling across the tortilla. Roll it up quickly and repeat the process until all the tortillas are filled.

Fry the rolled up tortillas in about 1/3 inch hot vegetable oil on both sides until they are crisp. Drain on paper towels and arrange on serving plates. Put a dollop of sour cream on each one and sprinkle with the remaining minced onion and crumbled cheese. Offer salsa. Makes 6 servings.

Pork Tacos los Robles

3 lb boneless pork roast, trimmed of fat
1 lb dried pinto beans (do not presoak)
4 C water
4 large garlic cloves, minced or pressed
2 T cumin seed
2 T chile powder
2 T dried oregano
1 t ground coriander
3/4 t cayenne pepper
1 can (28 oz) whole tomatoes (with juice)
1 can (7 oz) diced green chiles
1 T salt
1/2 t black pepper
2 doz flour tortillas (9-10 in), warmed
    condiments: grated Monterey Jack cheese, chopped olives, salsa, sour cream, guacamole,
    chopped lettuce and tomatoes

Preheat oven to 250. Place the pork roast in a large Dutch oven. Add the remaining ingredients and stir to mix well. Cover and bake for 7-8 hours or until beans are tender. Check the roast from time to time during cooking and add more water if mixture gets too dry.

When done, remove the meat from pan and shred in bite-sized pieces. Return the meat to pan and stir. (Should be consistency of chile con carne). Allow to stand before serving. Correct seasonings.

Place a warm tortilla on each serving plate. Have guests top with meat mixture and add a choice of condiments. Fold in edges and roll loosely. Serves 6-8.

Spicy Sirloin Steak Tacos

4 flour tortillas, warmed
1 tomato, seeded and chopped
1 small onion, chopped
3 pickled jalapeño chiles, seeded and chopped fine
    salt, to taste
1 small onion, thinly sliced
1 T vegetable oil
1/2 lb boneless sirloin steak, thinly sliced across the grain
1/4 C sour cream
3/4 C grated Monterey Jack cheese

In a small bowl, make the salsa by mixing together the tomato, chopped onions, jalapeños, the avocado and the salt. Set aside.

In a large skillet, cook the chopped onion in the oil over moderately low heat until softened.

Increase heat to moderate - high. Add steak and cook it, stirring constantly until liquid it gives is evaporated.

Divide sour cream among the tortillas, spreading it evenly. Sprinkle with the grated cheese and top with the steak. Divide salsa among tortillas and roll up enclosing the filling. Makes 4 soft tacos.

Turkey-Asparagus Soft Tacos

12 medium-size asparagus spears
6 flour tortillas (9-10 in) warmed
6 oz thinly sliced Monterrey jack cheese
3/4 lb thinly sliced cooked turkey breast, cut into strips
3 oz sliced, pickled jalapeño peppers

Snap off and discard tough ends of asparagus. In a deep 10 to 12 inch nonstick frying pan over high heat, bring about 1 inch water to boiling. Add asparagus; cook, uncovered, until barely tender when pierced, 3 - 5 minutes. Drain and immerse in ice water. When cool, drain and set aside.

Dry pan and set on medium heat. Lay tortillas in pan, 1 at a time (use 2 pans to speed cooking), and quickly top each with 1/6 of the cheese, turkey, asparagus spears, and peppers. Heat just until cheese begins to melt, about 1 minute; lift tortilla to fold in half over filling. Makes 6 servings.

Steak and Corn Tacos Picante

2 T olive oil
1 large onion, sliced
1 large red bell pepper, sliced
1/2 lb skirt (or flank) steak, cut into 1/4 inch long narrow strips
3/4 cup fresh or frozen whole kernel corn (cooked and drained)
2 jalapeño chiles, minced - with seeds
1/2 t chile powder
    salt and pepper
2 T fresh cilantro, minced
4-6 corn or flour tortillas (7-8 in), warmed
1/2 C grated cheddar cheese
    sour cream
    prepared salsa

Heat oil in heavy large skillet over medium heat. Add onion and bell pepper and sauté until tender - about 10 minutes. Transfer to plate.

Add steak to skillet. Stir until no longer pink - about 1 minute. Return onion and pepper to pan. Add corn, jalapeños, cumin and chile powder. Stir until heated through. Season with salt and pepper. Remove from heat and mix in cilantro.

Transfer to heated platter and keep warm.

Place warm tortillas in napkin-lined basket. Serve tortillas, steak, cheese, sour cream and salsa separately. Guests can assemble tacos at the table. This recipe may be doubled or tripled, as needed. Makes 4 - 6 tacos.

Chicken-Cilantro Soft Tacos with Tomatillo Sauce

5 poblano chiles, cut in 1/4 inch strips
1 T vegetable oil
1 T butter
1 medium onion, sliced
2 large cloves garlic, minced or pressed
2 large whole chicken breasts, cut into 1/2 X 2 inch strips
   juice of 1 lime
salt and pepper, to taste
1 t dried oregano
2 T minced fresh cilantro
8 corn tortillas (7-8 in), warmed
   condiments: chopped tomatoes, sliced ripe olives, guacamole, lime
      wedges, shredded lettuce, shredded Cheddar and Jack cheeses
   Tomatillo Sauce (Recipe follows)

Using tongs or a long-handled fork, char the chiles over an open flame until the skins are blackened - about 3-4 minutes - turning frequently. (May be placed in a broiler pan and broiled about 2 inches from the heat until skins are blackened, turning frequently. This will take about 15 minutes. Transfer chiles to a plastic bag, close tightly and let them steam for about 10 minutes. When cool enough to handle, peel and seed them. Cut into 1/4 inch strips.

In a 12 inch skillet, heat the oil and butter over a low flame. Add the chiles, onion and garlic and sauté very slowly for about 15 minutes. Increase the heat to moderately- high; add the chicken and sauté quickly until chicken is no longer pink and just springy to touch. Add the lime juice, salt and pepper, oregano and cilantro. Reduced the heat to low and continue cooking for 5 minutes. Serve immediately wrapped in warmed tortillas with Tomatillo Sauce and condiments. Makes 8 tacos.

Tomatillo Sauce:

3/4 lb fresh tomatillos, husks removed   1/2 t salt
3 cloves garlic, minced or pressed   2 jalapeño chiles, seeded and diced
1 medium onion, chopped   1 C fresh cilantro leaves, chopped
1/2 C regular strength chicken stock   3 T vegetable oil
1/2 t sugar

Wash the tomatillos and remove the stems. In the bowl of a food processor, place the tomatillos, garlic, onions, stock. sugar, salt, chiles and cilantro. Process until well blended. Heat the oil in a 12 inch skillet over moderate heat. Add the toma- tillo mixture, reduce heat and simmer for 10 minutes. Remove from heat. Serve heated or at room temperature. (May be made the day ahead and refrigerated until ready to use - it also freezes well).

Crab Tacos with Pineapple Salsa

2 T vegetable oil
2 cloves garlic, minced or pressed
1 medium onion, chopped
1 large tomato, chopped
1 can (4 oz) diced green chiles
1 lb cooked crab meat, shelled
1 doz corn tortillas (6-7 in), warmed
  Pineapple Salsa (recipe follows)

Heat oil in a 12 inch skillet over medium-high heat. Stir in garlic and onion and cook until onion begins to brown - about 10 minutes. Add tomato and chiles. Simmer until tomatoes are soft - about another 7 minutes.

Have guests spoon about 1/2 crab mixture onto a warmed tortilla. Add salsa and salt to taste. Fold in half and eat immediately. Makes 12 tacos.

Pineapple Salsa

1/2 C chopped cucumber
2 jalapeño chiles (stemmed, seeded and minced)
1 C diced pineapple
1 t grated lime peel
3 T fresh lime juice
2 T minced fresh cilantro

Mix together chopped cucumber, jalapeño chiles, pineapple, grated lime peel, fresh lime juice and fresh cilantro. Cover and refrigerate for at least one hour or up to two days.

Tuna Tacos with Yogurt and Mustard

1 can (6 1/2 oz) solid white tuna, drained and flaked
1/2 C plain yogurt
1 celery stalk, diced
1 t Dijon mustard
1/4 t dried dillweed
    freshly ground pepper, to taste
2 corn tortillas (6-7 inch), warmed
    iceberg lettuce, shredded
    sliced tomatoes

Combine the first 6 ingredients in a bowl. Divide between the 2 warmed tortillas. Top with lettuce and tomatoes, fold up and enjoy! Makes 2 tacos.

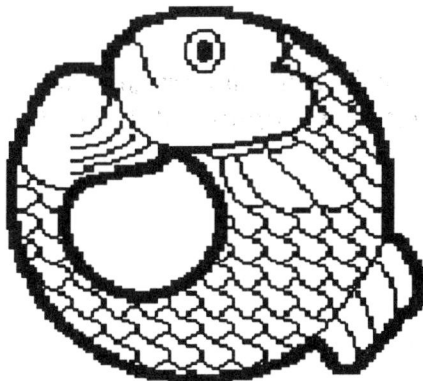

Fajitas de Pollo

3 T vegetable oil
1 large onion, sliced thinly
1 bell pepper, sliced thinly
1/4 t ground cumin
1/4 t chile powder
1/4 t cayenne pepper
1/4 t dried oregano, crumbled
1/4 t garlic powder
1/4 t dried thyme, crumbled
1/2 C chicken broth, full strength
4 boneless chicken breast halves, skinned, cut into strips
8 flour tortillas, (9-10 in) warmed
1 tomato, chopped
1 avocado, peeled and sliced
  salsa fresca or prepared salsa

Heat oil in heavy large skillet over medium-high heat. Add onion and bell pepper and sauté until almost tender - about 10 minutes. Add seasonings and continue cooking about 1 more minute.

Mix in broth and bring to boil. Add chicken and stir until cooked through - about 5 minutes. Spoon chicken mixture onto tortillas. Roll up. Top with tomato and avocado. Pass salsa separately. Serves 6.

Fajitas de Carnitas

1 pork shoulder, 5-6 lb
3 large carrots, chopped
2 large onions, chopped
1/2 t each ground cumin, thyme, oregano and chile powder
6 C water
12 oz prepared green chile salsa
1/2 C green onions, sliced (including tops)
1 can (7 oz) diced green chiles
   guacamole
   salsa fresca or prepared salsa
12 flour tortillas, (9-10in), warmed

Place pork in a 6 to 8 quart pan. Add carrots, onion, seasonings and water. Bring to a boil over high heat. Reduce heat, cover and simmer until pork is very tender - about 3 to 3 1/2 hours.

Lift meat from broth and place in a 9 x 13 x 2 inch pan. Bake, uncovered, at 350 until meat is well browned - about 45 minutes to one hour.

Drain off fat. When cool enough to handle, shred meat, discarding bones and pieces of fat.

Stir salsa, green onions and chiles into meat. Return to oven until hot - about 15 minutes.

To serve, spoon mixture onto tortillas and top with guacamole and salsa. Roll to enclose (as best as possible) and eat immediately. Makes 12 fajitas.

Marinated Chicken Fajitas

1 1/2 lb skinned chicken breasts, sliced into strips
1 1/2 t garlic salt
1 1/2 t ground cumin
1/2 t chile powder
1/2 t crushed red pepper flakes
2 T olive oil
1 T lemon juice
4 T vegetable oil
1 medium onion, sliced
1/2 C chopped green onions
l large red bell pepper, sliced
8 flour tortillas (9-10 in), warmed
2 large avocados, sliced
   prepared salsa
   sour cream

Marinate chicken slices with seasonings, olive oil and lemon juice.

Sauté onions and bell pepper in vegetable oil until lightly browned. Remove from skillet. Sauté marinated chicken about 4 minutes. Toss with vegetables.

Have guests spoon chicken onto warmed flour tortillas and add avocado slices, salsa and sour cream. Roll up and eat immediately. Makes 8 fajitas.

Flank Steak Fajitas

1 1/2 lb. flank steak
1/2 C vegetable oil
1/2 C sherry
1 T chile powder
2 cloves garlic, minced or pressed
2 t cumin
   salt and freshly ground pepper, to taste
8 flour tortillas (9-10 in), warmed
2 C shredded lettuce
1 lb sharp cheddar cheese, grated
6 green onions, chopped
   prepared salsa

Marinate steak in the oil, sherry, chile powder, garlic and cumin over night or at least 4 hours.

Broil or grill about 7 minutes, salt and pepper, to taste. Carve into thin slices across the grain. Have guests place several slices of meat on a warm tortilla - add lettuce, cheese, onions and salsa. Makes 6 fajitas.

Fajitas San Felipe con Pico de Gallo

1 T freshly ground pepper
1 T garlic salt
1/2 t onion powder
1/2 t cayenne
2 lb skirt steak, tenderized and trimmed
1 doz flour tortillas (9-10 in), warmed
   Pico de Gallo (recipe follows)
   guacamole

Combine spices and rub over the meat. Cover and refrigerate for at least 12 hours.

Prepare barbecue and grill steak to desired degree of doneness, turning frequently. Slice across the grain into thin strips. Divide among tortillas, placing strips in center of each. Top with Pico de Gallo and guacamole. Roll up and eat! Makes 12 fajitas.

Pico de Gallo

4 medium peeled tomatoes
2 roasted, peeled and stemmed jalapeño peppers
1 small sliced onion
1/2 C fresh cilantro leaves
2 cloves minced garlic
1/2 t salt

Combine the following in a food processor and chop fine: tomatoes, jalapeño peppers (remove seeds if less heat is desired) onion, cilantro leaves, garlic and salt. Cover and refrigerate overnight. Makes 3 cups.

Stir-fry Fajitas

4 T vegetable oil
1 lb lean beef steak (sirloin or top round, cut across the grain into 1/8 inch strips)
2 cloves garlic, minced or pressed
1 large onion, minced
3 fresh jalapeño chiles, stemmed, seeded and minced
1 large red bell pepper, stemmed, seeded and thinly sliced
2 t ground cumin
3 T fresh lime juice
1 t cornstarch
2 medium Roma tomatoes, diced
    salt and pepper, to taste
    lime wedges
    sour cream
1 large avocado, peeled, pitted and diced
8 flour tortillas, (9-10 in) warmed
    prepared salsa

Heat a large frying pan or wok on high heat. When hot, add 1 tablespoon oil and 1/3 of the meat. Stir-fry until meat is lightly browned - about 2 minutes. Use a slotted spoon to transfer meat to a bowl. Repeat until all meat is browned.

Add 1 more tablespoon oil to pan, then add garlic, onions, chiles and bell pepper. Stir-fry until onion is tender - about 2 minutes. Mix together cumin, lime juice and cornstarch. Add to pan. Also add meat and tomatoes. Sir-fry until mixture is hot and juices boil. Add salt and pepper to taste. Pour fajitas into a serving dish and garnish with lime wedges.

Spoon fajitas onto warmed tortillas. Add sour cream, avocado and salsa and roll up. Eat out of hand. Makes 4 servings.

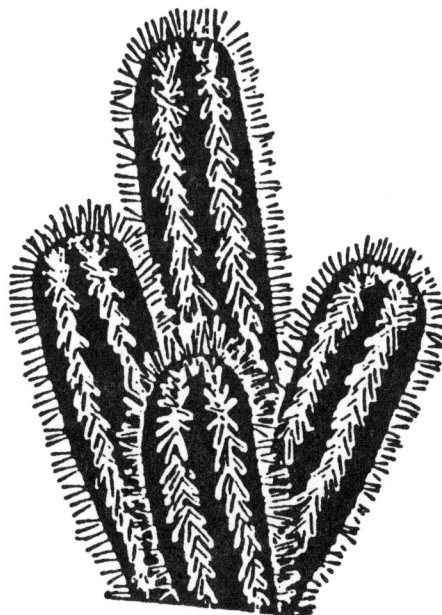

Grilled Fajitas with Tomatillo-Chile Salsa

2 t cumin seeds
2 large cloves garlic, minced or pressed
1 medium onion, thinly sliced
1/4 C fresh cilantro, minced
1 T chile powder
1 t dried oregano
1/4 C olive oil
2 T fresh lime juice

1 T soy sauce
1 T crushed red pepper flakes
3 1/2 lb flank steak
   salt and freshly ground pepper, to taste
   oil for brushing grill
8 flour tortillas (9-10 in), warmed
2 large avocados, peeled and diced
   Tomatillo-Chile Salsa (recipe follows)

Roast cumin seeds by placing them in a heavy, dry skillet heated over medium heat. Shake pan back and forth until the seeds become fragrant - about 12 minutes. In a small bowl combine cumin, garlic, onion, cilantro, chile powder, oregano, olive oil. lime juice, soy and red pepper. Whisk until well blended. Trim excess fat from steak. Place in a heavy plastic bag and pour the oil mixture over it and seal the bag. Place in refrigerator and marinate overnight. Turn the bag over several times every few hours.

Prepare the charcoal grill. Remove steak from bag. Brush off most of the marinade. When coals are white-hot, but not flaming, brush the grill with oil and place steak over coals. Grill to preferred doneness. (Four minutes per side for medium rare). Season with salt and pepper and transfer to a carving board. Cut thin slices across the grain. Have guests place several slices of beef on a warmed tortilla. Top with avocado and a spoonful of Tomatillo-Chile Salsa. Roll up and enjoy! Makes 8 fajitas.

Tomatillo-Chille Salsa

1 lb fresh tomatillos, husked and washed
6 sprigs fresh cilantro, roughly chopped
1 small onion, chopped
2 cloves garlic, minced or pressed
1 t olive oil
2 C chicken broth (regular strength)
salt and pepper, to taste

Cook tomatillos in boiling salted water until tender - about 5 minutes. Drain them. Place tomatillos and chiles in blender along with cilantro, onion and garlic. Blend until smooth, but still retaining a little texture. Heat oil in skillet over medium high heat - when oil is hot enough to make a drop of the purée sizzle sharply, pour the mixture in all at once and stir constantly for 5 minutes until mixture becomes dark and thick. Add broth and return to a boil. Reduce heat to medium and simmer until thick enough to coat a spoon - about 15 minutes. Season with salt and pepper. Makes 2 cups.

California Fajitas

1 1/2 lb flank steak
1/2 C fresh orange juice
3/4 C fresh lime juice
1/4 C tequila
3 green onions, minced
1 t salt
1 t Worcestershire sauce
4 large garlic cloves, minced or pressed
1/4 C vegetable oil
3/4 t chile powder
1/2 t black pepper
2 C grated Monterey Jack cheese
   Pico de Gallo (see recipe page 60)
1 doz flour tortillas (9-10 in), warmed

Place the meat in a large shallow glass dish. Make a marinade by mixing together the next 10 ingredients. Pour the marinade over the meat and marinate, covered, for 24 hours. Turn occasionally.

Bring the meat to room temperature before cooking. Grill the meat over hot coals for 3-4 minutes on each side, basting frequently with the marinade. Remove the meat to a carving board and let stand for 5 minutes before slicing. Slice the meat thinly across the grain.

Place the meat in warmed flour tortillas, topped with Pico de Gallo and the cheese. Roll or fold and eat immediately. Serves 6.

Burritos

Carne Adobada Burritos

16 dried red chiles (New Mexican)
5 cloves garlic, minced or pressed
1 T oregano, crumbled
1 t salt
1/4 C wine vinegar
4 lb pork tenderloin
1/2 C chicken broth
1 doz flour tortillas (10-12 in), warmed
    salsa fresca or prepared salsa

Rinse chiles under cold running water. Stem and seed and place in a large pot. Cover with water and simmer for 30 minutes.

Purée chiles in a blender in several batches. Use 1/4 cup cooking water with each batch. Add garlic, oregano and salt and blend.

Pour vinegar over the pork and then add half of the chile purée. Rub into the meat and let marinate, covered, in the refrigerator for at least 24 hours - but preferably for two to three days.

Place meat and its marinade in a Dutch oven, cover and roast at 325 for 1 1/2 hours. Stir in the chicken broth into the remaining chile purée and pour over the meat. Cover and cook for 30 minutes longer.

Let meat cool for 1/2 hour and then shred using two forks, or your hands.

Place 1/2 cup mixture onto each warmed tortilla. Fold over the four ends and place, seam side down, on a serving dish. Accompany with salsa. Makes 12 burritos.

Pork and Chile Burritos

3 lb boneless lean pork (cut in 1/2 inch cubes)
2 medium onions, minced
1 large green bell pepper, diced
1/2 bunch cilantro, chopped
2 medium tomatoes, chopped
2 cloves garlic, minced or pressed
3/4 T salt
1/2 t ground cumin
1/2 t ground cloves
1/2 t black pepper
2 bay leaves
3 jalapeño chiles, seeded and chopped
1 lb tomatillos
1 T fresh lemon juice
1/2 C cornstarch blended with 1 C water
1 doz flour tortillas (10-12 in), warmed
3/4 lb Monterey Jack cheese, shredded
3/4 lb sharp cheddar cheese, shredded

Place pork in Dutch oven and add 4 quarts water. Bring to a boil. Reduce heat and simmer, covered, for 40 minutes. Drain off water and add onions, bell peppers, cilantro, tomatoes, garlic, salt, cumin, cloves, pepper, bay leaves and jalapeños to meat.

Remove husks from tomatillos and boil in saucepan in 1 quart water until tender - about 15 minutes. Drain off water, mash tomatillos and add to meat mixture. Bring to a simmer and cook, stirring constantly for 15 minutes. Add lemon juice. Stir in cornstarch mixture, a little at a time, and continue simmering 15 minutes longer, stirring constantly.

To make burritos, place 1/2 cup meat mixture on each warmed tortilla. Fold over the four ends and place, seam side down, on a cookie sheet or a large baking dish. Sprinkle burritos with cheeses and place under broiler until cheeses begins to melt. Makes 12 burritos.

Piggy Burritos

1 lb lean boneless pork butt or shoulder, trimmed of excess fat
    and cut into 1-inch chunks
1 1/2 cups water
3 tablespoons ground chile powder
1 clove garlic, minced or pressed
3/4 t salt
1/2 t dried oregano, crumbled
1 T red wine vinegar
6 flour tortillas, (9-10 in), warmed
   sour cream
   salsa fresca or prepared salsa

Place meat in a 2-3 quart saucepan over medium-high heat and add water. Bring to a boil. Reduce heat, cover and simmer until meat is tender (about 1 hour).

Skim off excess fat. Add chile powder to pork along with garlic, salt, oregano and vinegar. Simmer uncovered, stirring occasionally, until sauce thickens (about 35 minutes).

Spoon onto center of warm tortillas and fold over the four ends. Place seam side down on individual serving plates. Top with sour cream and salsa. Makes 6 burritos.

Chicky Burritos

1 medium onion, chopped
1 clove garlic, minced or pressed
1 T vegetable oil
1 4-oz can chopped green chiles
1 10-oz can tomatoes
3 lb. fryer, cooked and boned
1 T chile powder
  salt and pepper, to taste
1 dozen flour tortillas (9-10 in), warmed
1 lb. Monterey Jack cheese, grated
  prepared salsa

In saucepan, sauté onions and garlic in oil until glazed. Add green chiles and tomatoes and bring to a boil. Lower heat and simmer for one hour.

Add chicken and mix until meat is well shredded. Season with chile powder, salt and pepper.

Place 1 1/2 to 2 tablespoons of the mixture on each warmed tortilla. Add a generous amount of cheese and salsa. Fold over the four ends and place, seam side down, in a greased 12 x 9 x 2 inch baking pan. Cover with foil.

Heat for about 20 minutes at 325. Place in individual plates and pass additional salsa. Makes 12 burritos.

Spinach and Cheese Burritos

1 pkg (10 oz) frozen chopped spinach, thawed
4 flour tortillas (9-10 in), warmed
1 T vegetable oil
1/2 lb mozzarella cheese, sliced
4 cloves garlic, minced or pressed
  salt and pepper, to taste
1 can (10 oz) enchilada sauce
  cilantro sprigs, optional

Squeeze moisture from spinach and set aside.

Place equal portion of cheese, garlic, then spinach in center of each warmed tortilla mounding ingredients onto one another. (Work quickly). Add salt and pepper, to taste. Fold over the four ends enclosing the filling and place, seam side down, in a baking dish.

Heat for about 15 minutes at 350. Meanwhile warm the enchilada sauce. Pour sauce evenly on 2 large dinner plates. Set 2 burritos on each plate. Garnish with cilantro. Makes 2 servings.

Beef Burritos with Creamed Peppers

1/2 lb flank steak
1 large clove garlic, minced or pressed
1/2 t cumin
1 1/2 t vegetable oil
1 1/2 t fresh lime juice
1 T olive oil
1 large onion, thinly sliced
2 Anaheim chiles, roasted ,peeled, seeded (cut in thin strips)
1 red bell pepper, roasted, peeled, seeded (cut in thin strips)
1/2 C whipping cream
3/4 C grated Monterey Jack cheese
1/2 t dried oregano, crumbled
   salt and pepper, to taste
1 T olive oil
4 flour tortillas (9-10 inch), warmed
1/2 C grated Monterey Jack cheese

Rub both sides of steak with garlic and cumin - then with 1 1/2 teaspoon vegetable oil and lime juice. Let stand for at least 2 hours.

Heat 1 tablespoon olive oil in heavy medium-sized skillet over high heat. Turn down and sauté onion until beginning to brown - about 6 minutes. Add chiles and peppers and stir until heated through. Add cream, then 3/4 cup cheese. Stir until mixture thickens - about 1 minute. Add oregano and season with salt and pepper.

Heat 1 tablespoon olive oil in large skillet over high heat. Season steak with salt and pepper. Cook until brown, about 2 minutes per side for rare.

Transfer meat to cutting board and halve across width - then against grain into thin slices. Spoon 1/4 cup mixture down center of each warmed tortillas. Fold over the four ends, enclosing filling, amd arrange in greased 5 inch baking pan, seam side down. Spread remaining mixture over tortillas and sprinkle with 1/2 cup cheese. Bake, uncovered, at 450 until cheese melts about 7 - 8 minutes. Makes 4 burritos.

Chorizo and Potato Burrito

1/4 lb new potatoes
2 T butter
2 scallions, sliced
1/2 lb chorizo (Mexican style)
 2 eggs, lightly beaten
1 flour tortilla (10-11in), warmed
1/4 C enchilada sauce
1/3 C Monterey Jack cheese, grated

In a saucepan combine the potatoes with enough cold water to cover them by 2 inches. Bring water to a boil and boil potatoes for 10 to 15 minutes - until tender. Drain potatoes and let them cool. Cut into 1/4 inch slices.

In a heavy skillet, heat 1 1/2 tablespoon of the butter, add the potatoes and cook them, stirring until they are golden brown. Transfer potatoes to a plate and keep warm.

Discard the casing from the chorizo and crumble. In a heavy skillet over moderate-high heat, sauté the scallions and the chorizo in the remaining 1/2 tablespoon butter. Stir frequently for about 5 minutes or until the chorizo is cooked through. Add the eggs and cook the mixture over moderate-low heat, stirring, until eggs are scrambled and incorporated well.

On a work surface, spoon the chorizo mixture down the center of the warmed tortilla. Top with the potatoes. Fold over the four ends enclosing the filling and place, seam side down, on a flameproof plate. Heat the enchilada sauce and spoon over it and top with the cheese.

Put burrito under a preheated broiler, about 4 inches from heat, for 30 seconds or until cheese is melted. Makes 1 burrito.

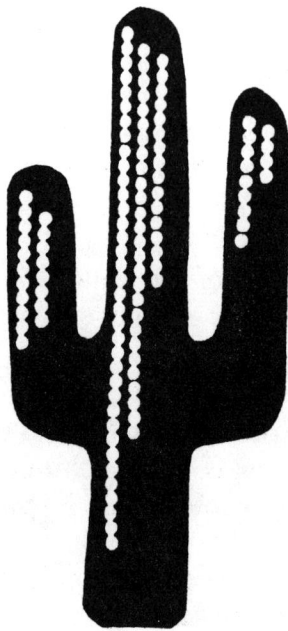

Quesadillas

Quesadillas Santa Ana

1 doz flour tortillas (10 in)
1/2 lb Monterey Jack cheese, grated
4 jalapeño peppers, thinly sliced
1 egg white, slightly beaten (if necessary)
 oil for frying
12 red leaf lettuce leaves
1 ripe tomato, diced
 guacamole

Place 6 tortillas on a work surface near the stove. Distribute cheese evenly over each tortilla - leaving a 1 inch margin around the edges. Sprinkle with sliced jalapeños and top with another tortilla. Seal edges, using a fork to crimp about 1/2 inch around each tortilla. (If tortillas do not seal properly - brush bottom edges with egg white so that they will stick together).

In a heavy frying pan (at least 12 inches in diameter) heat 1/2 inch oil to medium- hot. Fry tortillas, using 2 spatulas for turning and to avoid splattering, until each side is golden. Drain well.

To serve, cut each tortilla into sixths and serve immediately. Garnish with a lettuce leaf, tomato and guacamole. Makes 12 quesadillas.

Ham and Cheese Quesadillas

4 T butter, divided
8 flour tortillas (9-10 inch)
2 C Monterey Jack cheese, grated
1 can (4 oz) diced green chiles
1/2 C thinly chopped green onions
4 oz thinly sliced ham

Butter two cookie sheets using 1 tablespoon butter for each. Arrange two tortillas on each cookie sheet. Top each tortilla with 1/2 cup of the cheese. Sprinkle each with three tablespoons of the diced chiles and two tablespoons of the green onion. Top with remaining tortillas.

Melt remaining two tablespoons butter and brush tops of tortillas. Bake at 500 until cheese has melted and tortillas are golden brown about 10 minutes. Makes 4 quesadillas.

Crab Quesadillas

1/2 lb shelled cooked crab
2 C Monterey Jack cheese, shredded
1 C green onions, thinly sliced
10 flour tortillas (8-10 in)
    fresh cilantro sprigs
    Chile-Cilantro Sauce (recipe follows)

Mix crab, cheese and onions in a bowl. Place 5 tortillas in a single layer on two 14 x 17 inch baking sheets.. Evely cover tortillas with crab mixture to within 3/4 inch of edges. Top each with 1 of the remaining tortillas.

Bake at 450 until cheese melts and tortillas are lightly browned about 8 minutes. Slide tortillas onto a board and cut each into 6 wedges. Arrange on a platter and garnish with cilantro sprigs. Offer Chile-Cilantro Sauce to add to each serving. Makes 10 servings.

Chile-Cilantro Sauce

4 large anaheim chiles
1 small onion
2 T lemon juice
1/4 C white wine
1 C firmly packed cilantro
1/3 C melted butter

Place chilies on a 12 x 14 baking sheet and broil 2 inches below heat until brown and blistered on all sides. Turn often - about 5 minutes. Let cool and then remove skin, stems and seeds. Coarsely chop and place in a blender or food processor. Whirl with onion, lemon juice and white wine until smooth.

Pour into a 3 quart pan and bring to a boil over high heat, stirring, until reduced to 1/3 cup - about 8 minutes. Salt and pepper to taste. Return mixture to blender. Add cilantro and whirl until smooth. With motor running, slowly add hot melted butter until incorporated. Serve warm.

Mamalenche's Quesadillas with Tomatillo Salsa

1/2 lb tomatillos, husks removed and rinsed or 1 can (13 oz) tomatillos, drained
1/2 lb jícama, peeled and rinsed
2 fresh jalapeño peppers, stemmed, seeded and finely chopped
1/3 C fresh lime juice
8 flour tortillas (8-10 in)
1 lb Montery Jack cheese, thinly sliced
1/2 lb cooked ham, thinly sliced
2 t butter
1/2 C fresh cilantro leaves

Make the salsa by coring the fresh tomatillos and finely chopping them along with the jícama. Combine in a bowl with the jalapeños and lime juice. May be used immediately or covered and chilled up to overnight.

Lay 4 tortillas flat. Cover surface of each with an even layer of cheese and ham and put another tortilla on top. Press lightly to make them stick together. As quesadillas wait to be cooked, cover with plastic wrap to keep from drying.

Place a 12 inch skillet over medium heat. When hot, add 1/2 teaspoon of the butter to the pan and coat cooking surface. Using a wide spatula for support, place 1 quesadilla in pan. Cook until lightly spotted with brown on the bottom - about 3 minutes. Turn with spatula and cook until other side is lightly spotted with brown and cheese is melting. Remove from pan. Keep warm as remaining quesadillas are cooked. Cut into wedges. Accompany with the tomatillo salsa and cilantro. Makes 4 servings.

Red Pepper Quesadillas

3 T vegetable oil
1/2 medium onion, thinly sliced
8 flour tortillas, (8-9 in)
1 large red bell pepper, roasted, peeled and seeded (cut into 1/2 in strips)
6 oz mozzarella cheese, grated
6 oz Monterey Jack cheese, grated
2 cloves garlic, minced or pressed
1 t marjoram
1 t oregano
1/2 t salt
1/4 t black pepper
1/8 t cayenne pepper

Heat oil in skillet over medium heat. Add onion and sauté until soft and translucent, about 12 minutes. Mix together the onion with the bell pepper strips, cheeses and seasonings.

Heat skillet over high heat and soften tortillas by grilling for 30 seconds on each side.

Divide the mixture evenly over 4 tortillas and top with the remaining 4, pressing them down gently. Brush both sides with remaining oil. Bake quesadillas in preheated 400 degree oven for 3 to 5 minutes - or until lightly browned. Cut into quarters. Makes 4 servings

Quesadillas al Horno

4 flour tortillas, (7-8 in. wide), room temperature
   chile sauce, prepared
1/2 lb sharp cheddar cheese, shredded
2 Roma tomatoes, thinly sliced crosswise
1/2 C chopped onion
1/3 C fresh cilantro leaves, lightly packed
1/2 C prepared salsa

Lightly brush both sides of tortillas with water. Spread a little chile sauce on half of each tortilla. Evenly distribute 1/4 of the cheese, tomato, onion and cilantro over sauce. Fold plain half of tortilla over to cover filling.

Set quesadillas slightly apart on a 12 x 15 inch baking sheet. Bake at 500 until crisp and golden, 8-10 minutes.. With a spatula, transfer to plates. Offer salsa, if desired. Makes 4 quesadillas.

Chilaquiles

and

Chimichangas

Chicken Chilaquiles

1 doz corn tortillas (6-7 inch)
4 C chicken, boned, skinned, cooked
   tomatillo sauce (Recipe follows)
1 C sour cream
1/2 C whipping cream
4 C sharp cheddar cheese (shredded, firmly packed)
3/4 C grated parmesan cheese
1 large avocado, thinly sliced

Stack tortillas 6 at a time, and cut stack into 1/8 to 1/4 inch wide strips. Tear chicken into bite size pieces. Evenly pat half the chicken into a greased 9 x 13 x 2 inch baking dish. Spread with half the tomatillo sauce.

Stir together sour cream and whipping cream. Spread half the mixture over the tomatillo sauce. Evenly top sauce with 1/2 the tortilla strips and 1/2 the cheddar cheese.

Repeat layers using remaining chicken, sauce, cream mixture and tortillas. End with cheddar cheese.

Cover and bake at 350 for 40 minutes. Uncover and evenly sprinkle with the parmesan cheese. Continue baking until cheese is bubbly - about 10 minutes more. Remove from oven. Let stand 15 minutes. Arrange avocado slices on top. Cut into squares before serving. Serves 6.

Tomatillo Sauce:

In a blender or food processor, combine a 13 oz. can of tomatillos (including liquid), 1 large onion, quartered, 2 cloves garlic and a 4 oz. can of diced green chiles. Whirl until smooth.

David's Chilaquiles

2 doz day-old corn tortillas (7-8in)
3 T vegetable oil
2 cans (10 oz) tomatillos
2 small onions, chopped
3 serrano chiles, chopped
2 cloves garlic, chopped or pressed
1/2 C fresh cilantro
2 C Monterey Jack cheese, grated
3/4 C chicken broth
   salt and pepper, to taste

Cut tortillas into pie shaped pieces (about 6 per tortilla). Heat oil in a skillet and fry tortillas, a few strips at a time, on both sides, without browning. Add more oil, if needed while frying the tortillas.

Place the tomatoes, one chopped onion, chiles, cilantro and garlic in blender or processor and blend until smooth. Pour the mixture over the tortillas in the skillet. Simmer for five minutes.

Mix one half of the chopped onion with grated cheese. Sprinkle onion and cheese mixture over the top of the tortillas. Place skillet in oven at 350 until cheese is melted. Makes 6 servings.

Chilaquiles Gómez-Castro

2 doz day old corn tortillas (7-8 in)
3 T olive oil
2 cans tomatillos (10 oz each)
1 large onion, chopped
6 sprigs cilantro
4 chiles serranos, chopped
2 C cooked chicken, cut in bite-size pieces
   salt and pepper (to taste)
1 C heavy cream
2 C parmesan cheese, grated
   cilantro sprigs for garnish (optional)

Cut tortillas into pie shaped pieces (about 6 per tortilla). Heat oil in an oven proof skillet and fry tortilla strips without browning. Drain and set aside.

Drain tomatillos and reserve the liquid. Combine tomatillos, chopped onion, cilantro and chiles in a blender or processor and blend to a smooth pure.

In a saucepan cook pure for 5 minutes over moderate heat, stirring constantly. Pour the sauce and one half cup cream over the tortillas. Add the chicken, mixing it with the tortillas. Add salt and pepper, to taste. Pour the remaining cream over the top and sprinkle with the grated cheese. Bake at 350 for 30 minutes. Garnish with fresh cilantro. Makes 6 servings.

Chilaquiles with Mushrooms

8 day old corn tortillas (6-7 in)
   vegetable oil for frying
   salt, to taste
1 lb mushrooms
2 T olive oil
5 cloves garlic, minced or pressed
1/4 t thyme
1/4 t oregano
1/4 t chile powder
   salt and freshly ground pepper, to taste
2T vegetable oil
1 C green onions, sliced
1 lb tomatoes, peeled and puréed
1/2 C diced green chiles
3 T fresh cilantro, chopped
1/2 lb cheddar cheese, grated
3 eggs
1 C milk

Cut the tortillas into strips about 1 inch wide. Fry them in vegetable oil until they are crisp and golden. Drain them on paper towels and salt them lightly .

Wash mushrooms and slice them. Heat olive oil in a large skillet and sauté the garlic in it until it begins to color. Add the sliced mushrooms and toss them over medium-high heat until they have released their water and most of it has evaporated. Add thyme, oregano and chile powder and salt and pepper, to taste. Toss until seasonings are evenly distributed. Set aside.

Heat vegetable oil in a skillet and sauté the green onions in it for a few minutes. Add the tomatoes, chiles, cilantro a little salt and pepper. Cook over medium heat for 5 minutes. Add the mushrooms to the tomato sauce.

Lightly oil a large casserole and cover the bottom with 1/3 the tortilla strips. Sprinkle 1/3 the cheese over them and then 1/3 the tomato-mushroom mixture. Repeat the layers: tortilla strips, cheese and then the mixture.

Beat together eggs and milk and pour over the casserole. In order to allow the liquid to drain evenly - slip a knife through the top layer in a few places.

Cover and bake at 350 for 1/2 hour. Makes 6 servings.

Chimichangas Jalisco

1 lb lean ground beef
2 T vegetable oil
3/4 t salt
1/2 t freshly ground pepper
1/4 t thyme
1/4 t oregano
1/2 t chile powder
6 flour tortillas (9-10 in), warmed
   vegetable oil for frying
1/2 lb sharp Monterey Jack cheese, grated
   sour cream, shredded lettuce, guacamole and salsa

Sauté ground beef in 2 tablespoons vegetable oil over moderate heat until meat is no longer pink. Add salt, pepper, thyme, oregano and chile powder. Simmer for 5 minutes.

Fold over the bottom third of a tortilla to made a solid base. Spread 1/3 cup of the meat mixture on the solid base and roll the base and filling, one turn up, so that the fold is in the center and widest part of the tortilla. Now fold in each side of the tortilla and roll again, once or twice until you have a neat package. Fasten the seam with toothpicks. Repeat the process with the remaining tortillas.

Heat vegetable oil in a large heavy skillet to 400 degrees. Deep fry the tortilla packets, two or three at a time, until they are golden, turning - about 8 to 10 minutes. Drain well on paper towels.

Place on a large platter. Sprinkle with cheese and garnish with the lettuce, guacamole and the salsa. Makes 6 chimichanhgas.

Strawberry Chimichangas
(great for breakfast)

2/3 C ricotta cheese
6 oz cream cheese, softened
1/4 C sugar
1 t grated lemon rind
1/2 t cinnamon
4 flour tortillas (9-10 in)
2 t butter
2 t vegetable oil
1/4 C strawberry jam
    sour cream
    fresh strawberries

Combine ricotta cheese, cream cheese, sugar, lemon rind, and cinnamon. Mix well and set aside.

Soften the tortillas by placing them in a microwave oven between damp paper towels for 20-30 seconds or wrapping in foil and heating in the oven at 350 for approximately 10 minutes.

Place a quarter of the filling in the center of each tortilla. Fold 2 sides in and fold over to enclose filling.

In a medium sized skillet heat the butter and oil over medium heat. When hot, place the tortillas, seam side down, in the pan. Cook for 2-3 minutes or until golden brown. Turn and cook for 2-3 minutes more.

Top each with 1 tablespoon of the strawberry jam and a dollop of sour cream. Garnish with fresh strawberries. Serves 4.

(Blueberries, peaches, raspberries or apricots may be substituted for the strawberries. Use the corresponding fruit jam).

Tostadas

and

Tortas

Bacon and Egg Tostadas with Refried Beans
(Great for breakfast)

12 slices bacon (about 3/4 lb)
1 can (15 oz) refried beans
4 flour tortillas (9-10 inch)
2 t vegetable oil
1/2 lb cheddar cheese, grated
4 large eggs
1/2 C chopped green onions
    salsa roja (recipe follows)
    beans (optional)

Cut bacon into 1/2 inch wide pieces and cook in a 10 inch skillet over medium heat until crisp. Stir often. Drain on paper towels.

Place refried beans in a 1 1/2 quart pan and cook over low heat until hot; stir occasionally. (May be heated in microwave oven).

Immerse tortillas one at a time in warm water - drain briefly. Lay tortillas flat in 2 lightly oiled baking pans, each 10 x 15 inches, and bake at 500 until pale gold - about 4 minutes. (Lower oven temperature to 350 degrees).

Remove from oven and sprinkle 1/4 of the cheese and 1/4 of the bacon evenly around outer edge of each tortilla. (Be sure to cover edges of tortilla completely to prevent too much browning). Break an egg on top the center of each tortilla. Immediately return pans to oven and bake until eggs are set the way you like - 4 to 5 minutes for soft yolks with firm whites.

Carefully loosen tostadas from pan with a wide spatula. Transfer 1 tostada to each dinner plate. Spoon salsa roja, to taste, onto each tostada. Sprinkle with green onions. Accompany with beans. Serves 4.

Salsa Roja:

In a 12 inch skillet combine 2 tablespoons olive oil, 1 medium chopped onion and 2 minced or pressed cloves of garlic. Stir occasionally until onion begins to brown lightly - about 8 minutes. Stir in 2 tablespoons of chile powder, 1/2 teaspoon ground cumin, 1/4 teaspoon oregano, 1 can (15 oz) tomato purée and 1 cup regular-strength chicken broth. Bring to a boil, then reduce heat and simmer, uncovered, until reduced to 2 1/2 cups - about 25 minutes. Serve hot.

Tostadas-a-Go-Go

2 corn tortillas, (7-8 in)
2/3 C refried beans
4 thin slices avocado
1/4 C plain low-fat yogurt
2 T shredded Monterey Jack cheese
   shredded lettuce
2 T prepared salsa

Preheat oven to 375. Arrange tortillas on oven rack and bake until crisp - about 15 minutes. (May be heated in microwave on high power for about 3 minutes per tortilla.)

Heat beans. Spread beans on the tortillas and top with yogurt, cheese, lettuce and salsa. Makes 2 tostadas.

Ground Pork Tostadas

1 large onion, chopped
4 cloves garlic, minced or pressed
2 T olive oil
2 lb ground pork
1/3 C raisins
1 1/2 C tomato sauce
1/2 C sliced green olives
1/4 t cinnamon
1/4 t ground cloves
    salt and freshly ground black pepper, to taste
    vegetable oil (for frying tortillas)
1 doz corn tortillas (6-7 inch)
3 C iceberg lettuce, shredded
1 1/2 C red onion, thinly sliced
    salsa fresca or your favorite prepared salsa

Cook the onion and garlic in the olive oil in a heavy large skillet over moderately low heat. When the onion is softened, add the pork and cook over moderate heat, stirring, until the pork is no longer pink. Pour off any excess fat then add the raisins, tomato sauce, olives and spices. Simmer the mixture, stirring occasionally, for 15 minutes, or until it is thickened.

In a heavy skillet, heat 1/4 inch vegetable oil over moderately-high heat until it is hot but not smoking. Fry the tortillas, one at a time, for 30 seconds or until they are crisp and golden. Transfer them with tongs as they are fried to paper towels to drain.

Arrange the fried tortillas on individual plates. Divide the pork mixture on top of them. Top with the lettuce and the onions. Pass the salsa. Makes 12 tostadas.

Spinach-Flank Steak Tostadas

2 red bell peppers, seeded and chopped
2 jalapeño peppers, seeded and chopped
1 medium onion, chopped
2 medium tomatoes, diced
1/4 C red wine vinegar
3/4 C olive oil
1 1/2 lb flank steak
    salt and freshly ground pepper, to taste
1/4 C sunflower seeds
    vegetable oil for frying
1 lb fresh spinach, washed and shredded
6 corn tortillas (6-7inch)
1 C sliced ripe olives
1 C feta cheese, crumbled
2 T cilantro, chopped

Mix together chopped bell peppers, jalapeños, tomatoes, vinegar and olive oil. Place the flank steak in a glass dish large enough to hold it in one layer. Pour the sauce over the steak and turn several times until it is evenly coated. Marinate for at least several hours or up to 1 day in the refrigerator. Turn occasionally.

Place the sunflower seeds in a small skillet over medium heat and stir them until they are browned - about 2 minutes. Set aside.

Remove the steak from the dish and drain, reserving the marinade. In a large heavy skillet heat enough oil to coat the bottom. Fry the flank steak 3 minutes on one side, 2 minutes on the other, (or to desired doneness). On a cutting board, slice the steak across the grain into 1 inch strips . Place in a warming oven.

Bring the marinade to a boil in a small saucepan. Simmer for 5 minutes. Keep warm.

Crisp the tortillas by placing them in a hot skillet with a little oil for a minute per side.

Spread 1 cup shredded spinach over each crisped tortilla. Top with some steak strips. Arrange olive slices, cheese and sunflower seeds over the steak. Drizzle some warm marinade over the top and sprinkle with chopped cilantro. Makes 6 tostadas.

Gran Tostadas Arizona

4 flour tortillas (10 inch)
1 C sharp cheddar cheese
1 C Monterey Jack cheese
1 C provolone cheese
3 Anaheim chiles

Arrange single layers of tortillas on baking sheets and toast in a 500 degree oven for 5 to 7 minutes, until crisp and brown. Set aside.

Mix the 3 cheeses together and sprinkle 3/4 cup of the mixture evenly over each tortilla.

Cut chiles in narrow strips - about 1/2 inch long. Top each tortilla with chile strips.

Place in preheated broiler and broil until cheese melts - about 1 minute. Makes 4 tostadas.

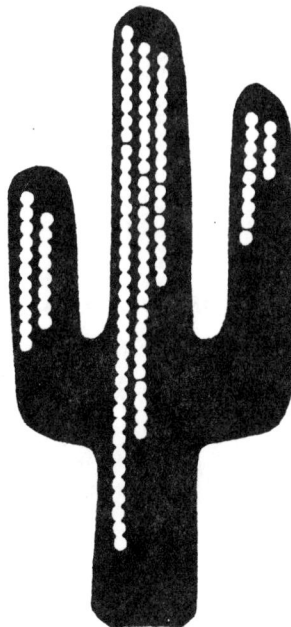

Tostadas de Huachinango
(Red Snapper Tostadas)

1/2 C vegetable oil
6 corn tortillas (6-7 in)
3 t chopped pickled jalapeño pepper
   (plus 1 t liquid from the jar)
1 lb cooked red snapper
   (any other lean white fish may be substituted)
1 medium onion, finely chopped
1 large tomato, seeded and cut into 1/2 inch dice
1/3 C olive oil
2 T fresh lemon juice
2 T chopped cilantro
   (additional cilantro for garnish)
1/2 t salt
1/4 t freshly ground pepper
1/3 C mascarpone cheese
2 C iceberg lettuce, finely shredded
1 large ripe avocado, sliced thinly

Heat the vegetable oil in a small skillet over moderately-high heat until hot - 2 to 3 minutes. Fry the tortillas, one at a time, turning several times with tongs until golden - about 2 minutes total. Drain on paper towels and set aside.

Chop and mash the jalapeño pepper until it becomes a paste. Set aside.

Flake the fish into a large bowl. Add the onion and toss gently. Add the jalapeño paste, jalapeño juice, tomato, olive oil, lemon juice and cilantro and toss very gently. Season with salt and pepper and set aside.

Spread each tortilla with a heaping teaspoon of mascarpone. Sprinkle some lettuce on top. Add the fish mixture, spreading it out a little to the sides. Top with the avocado slices and several sprigs of cilantro. Dollop the remaining mascarpone in the middle of each tostada. Makes 6 tostadas.

Soups

and

Salads

Classic Tortilla Soup

3 medium Anaheim chiles
2 T butter
2 T vegetable oil
2 large onions, thinly sliced
3 large garlic cloves, minced or pressed
2 medium jalapeño chiles, seeded and finely chopped
3 C chicken stock
1 can (28 oz) Italian plum tomatoes, coarsely chopped, liquid reserved
1/2 C tomato sauce
2 t chile powder
1 t ground cumin
1/2 t dried oregano, crumbled
   salt and pepper, to taste
1/2 C fresh cilantro, chopped
4 day old corn tortillas (7-8 in) cut into strips

Char Anaheim chiles over gas flame or in broiler until blackened on all sides. Transfer to paper bag and let stand 10 minutes to steam. Peel and seed; rinse under cold water and pat dry. Cut each chile into thin strips.

Melt butter with oil in heavy large skillet over low heat. Add onions and garlic and cook until softened but not brown, stirring occasionally, about 10 minutes.

Add Anaheim and jalapeño chiles and cook until tender, stirring occasionally, about 5 minutes. Transfer to large pot. Add stock, tomatoes with liquid, tomato sauce, chile powder, cumin, oregano, salt and pepper and bring to boil. Reduce heat and simmer 20 minutes to blend flavors.

Place some of the cilantro, tortilla strips and grated cheese in each of six bowls. Ladle soup over. Serve immediately. Makes 6 servings.

Tortilla Soup San Felipe

1 T vegetable oil
1 large onion, chopped
6 cloves garlic, minced or pressed
2 medium new potatoes, cubed
2 qt regular strength chicken broth
2 medium carrots, thinly sliced
2 stalks celery, thinly sliced
2 T tequila (may substitute gin)
1/2 t dry thyme leaves
1/2 t ground cumin
1/2 t dried oregano, crumbled
1 bay leaf
1/2 t liquid hot pepper seasoning
1/2 C fresh cilantro, chopped
8 corn tortillas (6-7 inch), cut into strips
1/4 lb Monterey Jack cheese, shredded
1/4 lb sharp cheddar cheese, shredded
    freshly made salsa fresca or prepared salsa

In a 6 quart pan, combine 1 tablespoon oil, onion and garlic on medium heat. Stir until onion is soft, about 8-10 minutes. Add potatoes, broth, carrots, celery, bell pepper, thyme, cumin, oregano, bay leaf and hot pepper seasoning. Bring to a boil. Reduce heat, cover and simmer until potatoes are tender when pierced with a fork, about 15 minutes. Stir in cilantro.

While potatoes are cooking, add about 1/4 inch oil to a 10-12 inch skillet over medium-hot heat. When hot, add tortilla strips, a portion at a time. Stir until crisp. Lift out with a slotted spoon and drain on paper towels. Repeat with remaining tortilla strips.

Place equal amounts of the tortilla strips and cheeses in individual soup bowls. Ladle soup into the bowls and pass the salsa. Serves 8.

Tortilla Dumpling Soup

8 stale corn tortillas (6-7 inch)
1 C milk
1 small onion, chopped
1 clove garlic, minced or pressed
1/4 C Parmesan cheese, grated
1/2 t oregano
1 egg, slightly beaten
2 egg yolks
  salt and freshly ground pepper, to taste
2 qt beef broth
1/2 C tomato purée
1/2 C cilantro, chopped

Soak the tortillas in the milk for 5 minutes. Place them in a blender with the onion and garlic and blend until smooth.

Combine the blended tortilla mixture with the cheese, oregano, egg and egg yolks, salt and pepper. Set aside.

Heat the beef broth and tomato purée. When it comes to a boil, lower heat to a simmer and drop in tortilla dumplings, one at a time, and poach for 10 minutes. Pour in bowls and garnish with chopped cilantro. Serves 6.

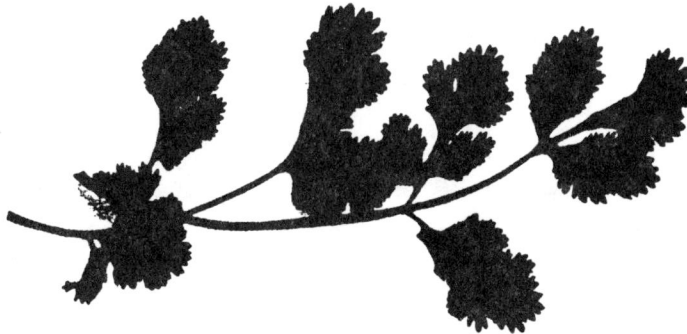

Sopa Tolteca

4 dried chiles anchos or pasillas
2 T vegetable oil
1 medium onion, minced
2 large cloves garlic, minced
2 T flour
6 C beef broth
1/3 C tomato paste
1/2 t dried thyme
1/2 t marjoram, crumbled
1 bay leaf
2 T minced parsley
    salt and freshly ground pepper
    oil (for frying tortillas)
8 corn tortillas (7-8 in), day old
1 1/2 C Monterey Jack cheese, grated
1 large avocado, diced

Put dried chiles in a small bowl and pour enough boiling water over them to cover. Set aside for 45 minutes to soften. (Turn twice during softening).

Heat 2 tablespoons oil in sauce pan. When very hot, add onion and sauté until soft. Add garlic and sauté 2 more minutes. Sprinkle with flour and sauté a minute longer - turning frequently. Remove from heat.

Remove largest of softened chiles from water. Reserve others for garnish. Pull stem off chile and discard. Open chile and remove seeds by washing it quickly under running water. Cut chile into chunks and put into blender with a little broth. Blend until smooth. Add puréed chile to onion mixture in pan along with remaining broth, tomato paste, thyme, marjoram, bay leaf and parsley. Mix well. Return soup to heat, cover and simmer gently for 1/2 hour. Taste and season with salt and pepper, as desired.

Cut tortillas into 1/4 inch strips. Pour 1 inch of oil into a heavy skillet. When very hot (a haze begins to form) add a few of the cut up tortillas and fry a minute or so until crisp and golden. Don't let them brown. Remove from oil and drain on paper towels while frying remaining tortillas.

Drain remaining chiles and discard stems, open and rinse off seeds. Cut into 2 1/2 inch chunks. Cover and reserve. Reheat soup to a boil before serving and add tortillas. Lower heat and simmer 3 minutes. Divide cheese among 6 soup bowls and spoon equal portions of tortillas into each. Fill bowls with soup. Add 1 chile chunk to each bowl and top with diced avocado. (Warn guests that chiles are very picante)! Serves 6.

Turkey-Tortilla Soup

4 corn tortillas (6-7 in) cut into strips
3 T vegetable oil
1 large onion, chopped
1 can (4 oz) diced green chiles
1 t chile powder
1 t ground cumin
1 large clove garlic, minced or pressed
1/4 t cayenne pepper
6 C chicken broth, regular strength
1 can (16 oz) tomatoes, coarsely chopped, reserve juices
1 lb boneless turkey breast cutlets, cut into 1 inch strips
1 large ear fresh corn, kernels cut from cob
    (or 1 C frozen whole kernel corn, thawed)
1/3 C fresh cilantro, chopped
   salt and freshly ground pepper, to taste
1/2 lb Monterey Jack cheese, grated

Heat 2 tablespoons oil in a large skillet and fry tortilla strips, a few at a time, until golden - about 1 minute per batch. Drain on paper towels. Repeat process until all strips are crisp.

Heat 1 tablespoon oil in a heavy large saucepan over medium-low heat. Add onion and sauté until translucent - about 4 minutes. Add chiles, chile powder, cumin, garlic, oregano and cayenne. Stir 1 minute.

Mix in the stock and the tomatoes and their juices. Bring mixture just to boil. Add turkey and simmer until cooked through - about 3 minutes.

Add corn and simmer 1 more minute. Mix in cilantro and season with salt and pepper, to taste.

Divide tortilla strips into four large soup bowls. Ladle soup into bowls. Sprinkle each serving with generous amount of cheese. Makes 4 servings.

Fresh Corn Soup

8 small ears fresh corn
1 C chicken broth
1/4 C butter or margarine
2 C milk
1 t cumin
1 clove garlic, minced or pressed
1 can (4 oz) diced green chiles
3 shakes cayenne pepper
1/2 t white pepper
1/2 t salt
8 corn tortillas (6-7 inch)
2 C vegetable oil
    salt, to taste
1 C Monterey Jack cheese, shredded
1 large tomato, diced
2 C cooked chicken, diced
1 C salsa fresca or prepared salsa
1/2 C sliced ripe olives
1 C sour cream
3/4 C green onions, sliced (use part of green)
1 large avocado, diced

Cut corn from cob and place in blender with the chicken broth. Process until smooth.

Melt butter in sauce pan. Add corn mixture and simmer for 5 minutes, stirring. Add milk, cumin and garlic. Bring to the boil. Add chiles and seasonings. Simmer, uncovered for 20 minutes.

Stack tortillas and cut into 1 inch pieces. Fry in hot oil (medium-high heat) until golden. Drain on paper towels, sprinkle with salt, to taste. Add cheese to soup and stir until melted.

When ready to serve, place 1/4 cup chicken and 1 tablespoon diced tomatoes in 8 soup bowls. Ladle soup into bowls and top each serving with tortillas, salsa, olives, sour cream onions and avocado. Serves 8.

Grilled Chicken Salad with Tortilla Chips

2 boneless whole chicken breasts (with skin), halved
1/2 C fresh lime juice
1 t dried oregano
   vegetable oil
4 corn tortillas,(9-10 in) cut into long thin strips
   salt
2 C cooked corn kernels
1 large red bell pepper, diced
4 green onions, thinly sliced
2 T fresh lime juice
1/2 t cumin
1/2 t thyme
1/4 C olive oil
1 bunch water cress, washed and spun dry

In a bowl let the chicken breast halves marinate in the lime juice with the oregano and salt and pepper to taste. Cover and chill for 30 minutes, at least.

Drain chicken, pat it dry and brush it with the oil. Grill the chicken, seasoned with salt and pepper on a well oiled rack set about 6 inches over glowing coals for 6-7 minutes per side until just cooked through. Transfer chicken to a cutting board and let stand for 10 minutes.

Make tortilla chips while chicken is grilling. In a heavy skillet heat 1/2 inch oil to moderate-high heat and in it fry tortilla strips in batches for about 1 minute - until they are golden brown. Transfer them with a slotted spatula to paper towels to drain. Sprinkle with salt.

In a large bowl, combine the corn, bell pepper and the green onions. Add the lime juice, cumin, thyme, oil and salt and pepper to taste. Toss mixture until well combined.

Cut chicken lengthwise into thin slices and add to the corn mixture with any accumulated juices.

Divide water cress and tortilla strips among 4 plates. Mound chicken salad in center of each plate. Serves 4.

Taco Salad Taxco

2 lb chicken breasts, skinned
2 C chicken broth
  juice of 1 lemon
4 corn tortillas (6-7 in), cut into triangles
2 t olive oil
1 small Romaine lettuce, torn into bite size pieces
1 small Boston lettuce, torn into bite size pieces
1 1/2 C cooked pinto beans (canned may be used but rinse well)
1 1/2 C cooked fresh corn kernels (frozen may be substituted)
1 1/2 C Mozzarella cheese, shredded
6 cherry tomatoes, halved
  Salsa Dressing (recipe follows)

Simmer chicken breasts in broth and lemon juice for 15 minutes. Remove pan from heat and let chicken cool in broth. W hen chicken is cool enough to handle remove meat from bones and cut into strips. Set aside.

Brush tortilla triangles with olive oil and arrange on a baking sheet in a preheated 350 oven. Bake for 8 to 10 minutes, or until crisp. Set aside.

Arrange equal portions of lettuce on each of 6 large dinner plates. Top with equal amounts of beans, corn, shredded cheese and chicken strips. Garnish with tortilla triangles and cherry tomatoes. Drizzle 2 tablespoons dressing over each and pass the remaining dressing at the table if desired. Makes 6 servings.

Salsa Dressing:

In a blender or food processor, place 3 tablespoons red wine vinegar, 3 tablespoons lemon juice, 1/4 cup water, 1/4 cup olive oil, 1 teaspoon Dijon mustard, 1 garlic clove, 1 pickled jalapeño pepper (from can), 1/4 cup chopped cilantro, salt and freshly ground pepper to taste. Blend well.

Cut 1 ripe tomato in half horizontally and squeeze out seeds and juice. Cut into pieces and add to blender. Roughly blend so bits of tomato remain. Pour into a jar and chill. (Keeps well in refrigerator up to 1 week). Makes 1 1/3 cup dressing.

Hors d'Oeuvres

Jalapeño Jelly Rolls

2 C cream cheese
1 jalapeño jelly
1 doz flour tortillas (8-9 in)

Blend the cream cheese and the jalapeño jelly together. Spread evenly on the tortillas.

Roll the tortillas, jelly-roll style, and refrigerate , covered with plastic wrap and a damp cloth, for at least 4 hours.

Before serving, cut in 1/2 inch slices and arrange on an attractive platter. Makes 50 rolls.

Variation:

Substitute 1 lb chopped ham, 1 can (7oz) green chiles and 1 can (7-8 oz) chopped black olives in place of the jalapeño jelly and proceed as above.

Tortilla Chips

1 doz corn tortillas
   water
1 t garlic powder
1 t chile powder

Heat oven to 375. Run tortillas, one at a time under the faucet. Shake off excess water each time. Sprinkle with seasonings. To cut, stack several tortillas on top of each other and cut into six triangles.

Arrange in a single layer on a baking sheet and bake in preheated oven until crisp - about 15 minutes. Do not overbrown. Makes 4 servings.

Tostaditas con Guacamole

3 corn tortillas (7-8 in)
   vegetable oil (for frying tortillas)
1 avocado, firm ripe
1 T fresh lime juice
2 T onion, finely chopped
1 clove garlic, minced or pressed
1 jalapeño chile, seeded and chopped
2 T fresh cilantro, minced
1/4 C tomato, finely chopped
   cilantro leaves for garnish

Cut each tortilla into 4 rounds with a 2-2 1/2 in. cutter. Arrange rounds in one layer on baking sheet. Cover them with a kitchen towel. Let stand for 1 hour.

In large heavy skillet heat 3/4 in. of the oil to medium heat and in it fry rounds in batches for 30 seconds to 1 minute, or until they are crisp and most of the bubbling subsides. Transfer chips with a slotted spoon to paper towels to drain. Sprinkle with salt. (Chips may be made several days in advance, but keep in an airtight container).

Peel and pit avocado and in large bowl mash coarse with a fork. Add lime juice, onion, garlic, jalapeño, cilantro and the tomato. Salt to taste. Stir mixture until well combined.

Top each tortilla chip with about 1 tablespoon of the avocado mixture and garnish with cilantro leaves. Makes 12 hors d'oeuvres.

Blue Cheese Beignets

1 C blue cheese, crumbled (room temperature)
2 t egg yolk
1 doz flour tortillas (7-8 in)
1 C all-purpose flour
2 T cornstarch
1 t baking powder
1/2 t salt
2 eggs
1 egg yolk
1/2 C water
2 t vegetable oil
   vegetable oil for frying
2 C unsweetened applesauce, chilled

Cream together the blue cheese and the 2 teaspoons egg yolk. Place one tortilla on a work surface and spoon a teaspoon of filling in the center. Fold the top, then the bottom, overlapping them to enclose the filling completely. Fold in the two remaining sides, overlapping them to make a square packet. Pinch the edges lightly to seal. Place seam-side down on a flat baking sheet. Repeat the procedure, arranging the packets in a single layer. Cover with plastic wrap and refrigerate for at least three hours or overnight.

Sift together the dry ingredients. Whisk the eggs, egg yolk, water the two teaspoons of vegetable oil in another bowl until smooth. Gradually stir the egg mixture into the dry ingredients, mixing just until smooth.

Heat four inches of oil in a heavy saucepan to 375. Dip four packets, one at a time, into the batter. Turn them with two forks until evenly coated. Let the excess batter drip off into the bowl. Slide the packets into the hot oil and fry, turning occasionally, until golden and puffed- about four minutes. Let drain on paper towels. Repeat the procedure with the remaining packets. Serve immediately with applesauce. Makes 12 beignets.

Desserts

Bananas Ballou

2 lb bananas, slightly green
6 T butter or margarine
2 T brown sugar
6 corn tortillas (7-8 inch)
2/3 C sliced almonds
1 1/2 C sour cream

Peel bananas and cut into 1/4 inch slices. Melt 2 tablespoons of the butter in a large heavy skillet over medium - high heat until foaming. Add the banana slices and brown on both sides - about 1 minute. Remove from heat and set aside in a bowl.

Add 1 tablespoon butter to the skillet over medium - high heat. Add 1 tablespoon of the brown sugar and heat until butter foams and the sugar melts. Place a tortilla in the pan and fry for 30 seconds turn and fry the other side. (Tortilla should be warmed through but still pliable). Remove and repeat process adding a little butter and sugar, as needed. Keep warm.

Toast the almonds in an ungreased skillet until toasted - about 3 minutes.

Stir together the sour cream and the powdered sugar in a small bowl.

When ready to serve, spread about 1/3 cup of the bananas on each tortilla. Top with the sour cream and sugar mixture. Dot with sliced toasted almonds. Fold in half. Serves 6.

Coffee Ice Cream Sundae Adelina

6 tostada cups (recipe follows)
1 qt coffee ice cream
1/4 C coffee liqueur

Scoop the ice cream into the center of the tostada cups. Top with some coffee liqueur. Serves 6.

Tostada Cups:

3 T butter or margarine
6 T granulated sugar
6 flour tortillas (8-9 inch)

In a large heavy skillet (large enough to hold a tortilla) place 1/2 tablespoon of the butter and 1 tablespoon of the sugar. Stir over medium heat until butter foams and sugar melts. Add a tortilla to the skillet until it puffs - about 1 minute. Turn and fry on the other side until browned - about a minute more. Remove the tortilla to a small bowl, pressing down the center to fit the bowl's shape. Let cool until set and then remove the tostada cup. Repeat the process. Makes 6 tostada cups.

Strawberry Sherbet Cha Cha Cha

6 corn tortillas (6-7 inch)
3 T butter or margarine
6 T granulated sugar
1 qt strawberry sherbet
1 basket (8 oz) fresh strawberries
1/2 C chopped pecans

Stack the tortillas and cut into 6 triangles.

Place 1/2 tablespoon of the butter and 1 tablespoon of the sugar in a large heavy skillet. Set over medium heat until the butter foams and the sugar melts. Add as many tortilla triangles as will fit without overlapping. Fry until they puff up - about 1 minute. Turn and fry on the other side until golden - about a minute longer. Remove to a platter, do not overlap. Add more butter and sugar to the pan and continue the process until all the triangles are golden and crisp.

Arrange three scoops of ice cream on each of 6 individual plates. Arrange 5 or 6 strawberries on each plate. Tuck in 8 or 9 tortilla chips around the scoops of ice cream. Sprinkle with chopped pecans. (An assembly line is helpful to insure presentation of this dish before the ice cream melts)! Serves 6.

Lemon Curd Tostadas

salad oil
6 flour tortillas (6 to 7 in. diameter)
3/4 C whipping cream
   lemon curd, recipe follows
6 medium strawberries

In a 4 quart pot, heat 1 1/2 inches salad oil to medium-high heat. Float 1 tortilla on top of the oil. Using the bowl of a metal ladle, press down on the center of the tortilla until it touches the bottom of the pan and bubbles up around tortilla edges. Hold tortilla down with ladle until it is golden brown and has formed a crisp bowl about 2 minutes. Lift tortilla from oil with tongs. Drain over a pan. Repeat process.

In a small bowl, beat whipping cream unti it holds soft peaks.

In another bowl, stir lemon curd with a spoon until smooth. Fold into whipped cream. Cover and chill until ready to use.

Set tortilla bowls on dessert plates and spoon about 1/3 cup of the lemon curd into each. Garnish with strawberries. Makes 6 servings.

Lemon Curd:

1/8 lb butter
1/2 t grated lemon peel
1/4 C sugar
2 large eggs

In the top of double boiler melt butter. Add lemon peel, juice, sugar and well beaten eggs. Whisk until blended. Cook over simmering water, stirring, until thickened and smooth - about 20 minutes. Cool, cover and chill until cold - at least 2 hours or up to one week. Makes one cup.

Russian River Fruit Cups

1/2 C raspberries
1/2 C blackberries
1 medium banana
1/2 C melon balls (cantaloupe or honeydew)
1 T lemon juice
1 carton (8 oz) plain yogurt
1 T honey
6 tostada cups (follow recipe page 118.)
  toasted coconut

Removed stems from berries. Slice the banana diagonally. Combine fruits and sprinkle with lemon juice to prevent darkening.

Stir together the yogurt and the honey.

Set tostada cups on dessert dishes. Fill each cup with about 1/4 cup fruit filling. Top with the yogurt sauce. Add a little more fruit filling and sprinkle with toasted coconut. Makes 6 servings.

Jacinto's Easy Banana Especial
(Cinnamon Tortillas filled with Banana Ice Cream)

8 flour tortillas, (8-9 in)
6 C vegetable oil (not prevously used)
1 T cinnamon
1/2 C sugar

1 qt banana ice cream
  (may substitute any flavor of your choice)
2 medium bananas, ripe but firm
juice of one lemon
1 C caramel sauce
  (chocolate or raspberry sauce may be substituted)

Using a cookie cutter or an inverted bowl, cut tortillas into rounds 4-6 inches in diameter. Heat the oil to 350 degrees. Place a tortilla in the oil and press the center gently down into the hot oil to form a shallow bowl. Fry until golden. Drain on paper towels. Repeat the process. Sprinkle the tortillas with cinnamon and sugar and set aside.

Peel the bananas and cut them into 1/2 to 1 inch pieces. Sprinkle with lemon juice to prevent discoloring. Set aside.

When ready to serve, pour the sauce onto 8 dessert plates. Place a tortilla on the sauce. Place several scoops of ice cream on each tortilla. Garnish with the bananas. Serves 8.

Tortillas

Flour Tortillas

2 C all-purpose flour
1/4 C cold vegetable shortening, cut into pieces
1 t salt

In a bowl blend the flour and the shortening until mealy. In a small bowl stir together salt and 2/3 cup warm water. Add the salted water to the flour mixture. Toss the mixture until liquid is incorporated. Form the dough into a ball and knead it on a lightly floured surface for 2 to 3 minutes or until it is smooth.

Divide the dough into 12 equal pieces. Form each piece into a ball. Cover with plastic wrap and let the dough stand for 30 minutes to an hour.

Heat a griddle over moderately high heat until it is hot. On a lightly floured surface roll 1 of the balls of dough into a 7 inch round. Cook the tortilla on the griddle for 1 to 1 1/2 minutes - turning once or until it is puffy and golden on both sides. Wrap tortilla in a kitchen towel and repeat process with remaining dough. Stack and enclose tortillas in the towel until all are done. Wrap tortillas in the towel and then in foil. Keep warm in a low oven up to one hour. Makes 12 tortillas.

Corn Tortillas

2 C dehydrated masa harina (corn tortilla flour)
1 C warm water

Stir flour with the warm water to make a dough that holds together but is not sticky. Shape into a smooth ball. Wet hands and divide the dough into 12 sections (keep moistening your hands as you shape the balls). Cover with plastic wrap to prevent dough from drying and let stand, covered, for 15 minutes.

Heat ungreased heavy skillet (or comal) to 475 to 500 degrees. With damp hands, pat one ball evenly with your hands and place it between two pieces of plastic wrap. Using the bottom of a pie pan, press to form a circle (use a rocking motion until a 6 inch circle is formed). Carefully peel off the plastic wrap. Cook on the preheated skillet for 30 seconds - turn and cook for 1 minute. Turn and continue to cook for another 30 seconds or so. Tortillas should be soft and pliable, but contain visible brown specks. Repeat the process. Stack the tortillas as you go, covering them and keeping them warm. Makes 12 tortillas.

Roasting and Peeling Peppers
(whether sweet bell peppers or the most fiery chile peppers)

Use a long-handled fork or tongs and char the peppers over an open flame (gas burners or a barbeque). Turn them, for 3 to 4 minutes until they are blackened completely. (Peppers may also be roasted on a heavy skillet on an electric stove). Transfer the peppers to a heavy, covered pot or place them in a plastic bag and seal tightly. Allow them to steam for 10 minutes. Keeping the peppers whole, peel them, starting at the blossom end. Cut off the tops and discard the seeds. (Some may prefer to wear rubber gloves when handling hot chiles).

Peppers may also be broiled on the rack of a broiler pan under a preheated broiler. Place peppers 2 inches from the heat and turn them every 5 minutes for 15 to 25 minutes, or until the skins are blistered and charred.

Warming Tortillas

Tortillas may be warmed in the following manners:

1. Place them in a single layer on HIGH in a microwave oven for about 40 seconds or until they begin to puff.

2. Stack tortillas in a clean, heavy towel and place in a steamer over 1/2 inch water. Cover and bring to a boil over medium-high heat. When steam becomes puffing out from under the lid - time for 1 minute, then remove from the fire and let stand 15 to 20 minutes. (Held in a very low oven, the tortillas will stay warm and moist for an hour or more.

3. Heat a heavy ungreased skillet until hot but not smoking. Cook tortillas for 10-15 seconds or until they begin to puff. Turn and briefly heat the reverse side.

Storing Cilantro

Wash the cilantro (or parsley). Shake off as much water as possible and place in a glass jar. Cover tightly and refrigerate. Every few days drain any water that may have accumulated in the bottom of the jar. Cilantro will stay fresh and green for several weeks.

Salsa Fresca

1 small onion, chopped
2 medium tomatoes, chopped
2 jalapeño peppers, finely chopped
1/2 t salt

Combine all ingredients. Serve immediately or may be refrigerated, covered, for up to 2 days. Makes 1 1/2 cups salsa.

Chile Fans

(Use to decorate your serving plates or platters)

2 red serrano, jalapeño or other small chiles
2 green serrano, jalapeño or other small chiles

Using a small sharp knife and starting just below the stem end, make lengthwise cuts down length of chiles - spacing cuts 1/8 inch apart. Carefully scrape out the seeds. Place chiles in a bowl of cold water and place bowl in the refrigerator Let stand at least 15 minutes or up to 1 day. Drain and pat dry before using. Makes 4 fans.

Avocado Fans

2 large firm-ripe avocados
juice of 1/2 lemon

Cut avodacos in half lengthwise. Remove and discard pits and peel. Set each avocado, cut side down, on a plate or platter. Starting at the large end of the avocado, make lengthwise cuts to within 3/4 inch of the top - spacing cuts about 1/2 inch apart. Press gently down on cuts to fan slices slightly apart. Sprinkle with lemon juice. Makes 4 fans.

Try *Salsa de Lorenzo* and *Tomatillo Salsa de Lorenzo* from Kozlowski Farms in Forestville, California in recipes calling for prepared salsa.

ADOBADO - marinated

ANAHEIM CHILE - a mild pepper, green to red in color which is about 3 to 5 inches long.

ACHIOTE - a seed from which achiote paste is made, the flavor is similar to chile powder and it give a rich color to sauces.

AGUACATE - avocado or alligator pear.

ANCHO CHILE - the dried version of the poblano chile (a fairly hot pepper).

BURRITO - a large (usually flour) tortilla containing a filling which usually includes beans. The tortilla is folded, envelope style, with the ends tucked in.

CARNE - meat

CARNE GUISDADA - roast meat.

CARNITAS - pork which has been cooked, usually, in its own fat.

CHILE POWDER - spice made from a combination of various peppers.

CHIPOTLE - smoked dried jalapeño chiles, very hot!

CILANTRO - sometimes called chinese parsley or coriander - it has a distinct pungent flavor and fragrance.

CHORIZO - pork sausage, the Mexican version hot and spicy and the Spanish version more mild.

CHILE VERDE - green chile, usually referring to a sauce made with tomatillos (Mexican green tomatoes).

COMAL - the original Mexican tortilla griddle.

CON - with

DE - of

ENCHILADAS - warmed soft tortillas wrapped around a filling and served with a sauce.

FAJITAS - soft tacos made with barbequed meats.

FLAUTAS - "flutes", crisp rolled tacos with guacamole topping.

FRESNO CHILES - a medium-hot pepper, green to red in color and about 3 inches long.

FRIJOLES - beans (dried).

FRIJOLES REFRITOS - refried beans.

GREEN CHILES - a very mild California pepper with only a faint bite.

GUACAMOLE - sauce which is a mixture of avocado, tomatoes, onions, cilantro and hot peppers.

GUAJOLOTE - turkey (pavo in Spain)

HUACHINANGO - Red Snapper (the variety off the pacific coast of Mexico is smaller and has a more delicate flavor than the rock fish from the California coast.)

HARINA - flour.

HORNO - oven.

JALAPENO - a moderate to hot chile pepper, about 2 inches long.

MASA - dough.

MASA HARINA - corn treated with lime water and specially ground to a very fine meal, (corn meal or polenta are much coarser and should not be substituted).

METATE - vessel (usually of stone) used in the grinding of corn.

PAPAS - potatoes ("patatas" in Spain).

PASSILA CHILE - fairly hot, about 4 inches in length.

PEPITAS - pumpkin seeds.

PICANTE - hot, as in spicy hot.

PICO DE GALLO - a salad that usually contains oranges, literally "rooster's beak").

POBLANO CHILES - fairly hot peppers, about 4 inches in length.

PULQUE - a fermented drink made from the agave (century) plant.

QUESADILLAS - cheese turnovers made with tortillas, developed after the Spaniards introduced goats to the New World.

QUESO FRESCO - a Mexican soft cheese.

SALSA - any sauce, but in California cuisine it has come to be known as a combination of chile peppers and other ingredients.

SALSA FRESCA - sauce made with only fresh ingredients, usually tomatoes, onion, cilantro, garlic and jalapeños.

SERRANO CHILES - moderately hot, about 3 to 4 inches in length.

SOPA - Soup

TACOS - tortillas folded over a filling. They are sometimes soft and sometimes fried crisp and are eaten like a sandwich.

TOMATILLOS - similar to green tomatoes with a parchment-like outer skin and having a fresh, tart flavor.

TORTAS - tarts or cakes.

TORTILLERA - Woman who makes tortillas.

TOSTADAS - fried flat tortillas heaped with various ingredients and served open face.

Acapulco Casserole, 23
Avocado Fans , 128
Bacon and Egg Tostadas, 94
Bananas Ballou, 116
BEEF:
 Beef Burritos with Creamed Peppers, 72
 California Fajitas, 63
 Chimichangas Jalisco, 89
 Fajitas San Felipe con Pico de Gallo, 60
 Flank Steak Fajitas, 59
 Grilled Fajitas with Tomatillo-Chile Sauce
 Ground Beef Bake Sonora, 13
 Ground Beef Enchilada Casserole, 8
 Microwave Enchiladas, 41
 Shredded Beef Enchiladas, 29
 Sour Cream Enchilada Casserole, 11
 Spicy Sirloin Steak Tacos, 50
 Spinach-Flank Steak Tostadas, 96
 Steak and Corn Tacos Picante, 52
 Stir Fry Fajitas, 61
 Tacos de Carne Guisada, 45
 Tortilla "Lasagne", 1
 Tortilla "Manicotti", 21
 Tortilla-Tamale Pie, 12
Blue Cheese Beignets, 113
Breakfast Enchiladas, 35
BURRITOS:
 Beef Burritos with Creamed Peppers, 72
 Burritos Italianos, 74
 Burritos de Papas, 71
 Carne Adobada Burritos, 67
 Chicky Burritos, 70
 Chorizo and Potato Burritos, 73
 Piggy Burritos, 69
 Pork and Chile Burritos, 68
 Spinach and Cheese Burritos, 69
California Fajitas, 63
Carne Adobada Burritos, 67
CHICKEN;
 Chicken Breast Montecito, 5
 Chicken and Cheese Celaya, 6
 Chicken-Cilantro Soft Tacos ,53
 Chicken Chilaquiles, 85
 Chicken Enchiladas Verdes, 32
 Chicken Enchiladas with Rum Sauce, 39
 Chicken-Yogurt Enchilada Casserole, 4
 Chickey Burritos, 68
 Chinese Enchiladas, 40
 Creamy Chicken Enchiladas, 33
 J.A.'s Chicken Casserole, 7
 Fajitas de Pollo, 56
 Grilled Chicken Salad, 107
 Marinated Chicken Fajitas, 58
 Tortilla-Chicken-Cheese Bake, 3
Chickey Burritos, 68
CHILAQUILES;
 Chicken Chilaquiles, 85
 Chilaquiles Gomez-Castro, 87
 Chilaquiles with Mushrooms, 88
 David's Chilaquiles, 86

CHIMICHANGAS:
 Chimichangas Jalisco, 89
 Strawberry Chimichangas, 90
Chorizo and Potato Burritos, 70
Classic Tortilla Soup, 101
Coffee Ice Cream Sundae Adelina, 122
Corn Tortillas, 123
Crab Quesadillas, 79
Crab Tacos with Pineapple Salsa, 54
David's Chilaquiles, 86
DESSERTS:
 Bananas Ballou, 117
 Coffee Ice Cream Sundae Adelina, 118
 Jacinto's Easy Banana Especial, 122
 Lemon Curd Tostada, 120
 Russian River Fruit Cups, 121
 Strawberry Sherbet Cha-Cha-Cha, 119
Eggplant "Lasagne", 18
ENCHILADAS:
 Breakfast Enchiladas, 35
 Chicken Enchiladas Verdes, 32
 Chicken Enchiladas with Rum Sauce, 39
 Chinese Enchiladas ,40
 Creamy Chicken Enchiladas, 33
 Enchiladas Coloradas, 27
 Enchiladas de Guajolote, 30
 Enchiladas Oaxaqueñas, 31
 Enchiladas with Salsa Verde, 28
 Enchiladas Suizas with Spinach, 34
 Microwave Enchiladas, 41
 Shredded Beef Enchiladas, 29
 Spinach-Raisin Enchiladas, 36
 Tex-Mex Enchiladas, 37
 Turkey-Asparagus Enchiladas Divan, 38
FAJITAS:
 California Fajitas, 63
 Fajitas de Carnitas, 57
 Fajitas de Pollo, 56
 Fajitas San Felipe con Pico de Gallo, 60
 Flank Steak Fajitas, 59
 Grilled Fajitas ,62
 Marinated Chicken Fajitas, 58
 Stir Fry Fajitas, 61
FISH AND SHELLFISH:
 Crab Quesadillas, 79
 Crab Tacos with Pineapple Salsa, 54
 Tacos de Huachinango, 46
 Tostadas de Huachinango, 98
 Tuna Tacos with Yogurt and Mustard, 55
Flautas, 48
Flour Tortillas, 124
Fresh Corn Soup, 107
Gran Tostadas Arizona, 97
Grilled Chicken Salad, 108
Ground Pork Tostadas, 95
Ham and Cheese Quesadillas, 78
HORS D'OEUVRES:
 Blue Cheese Beignets, 113
 Jalapeño Jelly Rolls, 111
 Tortilla Chips, 113

Jacinto's Easy Banana Especial, 122
Jalapeño Jelly Rolls, 111
Tostaditas con Guacamole, 115
J.A.'s Chicken Casseole, 7
Lemon Curd Tostadas, 115
Mamalenche's Quesadillas, 80
Marinated Chicken Fajitas, 58
Microwave Enchiladas, 41
Pinto Bean Soup, 106
PORK:
 Bacon and Egg Tostadas, 94
 Carne Adobada Burritos, 66
 Chinese Enchiladas ,40
 Chorizo and Potato Burritos, 73
 Ground Pork Tostadas, 95
 Ham and Cheese Quesadillas, 78
 Fajitas de Carnitas, 57
 Mamacita's Quesadillas, 80
 Pork and Chile Burritos, 65
 Pork Tacos los Robles, 49
 Tortilla Crust Casserole, 15
QUESADILLAS
 Crab Quesadillas, 78
 Ham and Cheese Quesadillas, 78
 Mamalenche's Quesadillas ,80
 Quesadillas al Horno, 82
 Quesadillas Santa Ana, 77
 Red Pepper Quesadillas, 81
Roll 'em up Red Bean Casserole, 16
Russian River Fruit Cups, 125
SALADS:
 Grilled Chicken Salad ,107
 Taco Salad Taxco, 108
SALSAS AND SAUCES:
 Chile-Cilantro Sauce, 79
 Pico de Gallo, 60
 Pineapple Salsa, 60
 Salsa Colorada, 27
 Salsa Dressing, 109
 Salsa Fresca, 128
 Salsa Roja, 94
 Sweet and Sour Sauce, 40
 Tomatillo-Chile Salsa, 62
SOUPS:
 Classic Tortilla Soup, 101
 Fresh Corn Soup, 106
 Sopa Tolteca, 104
 Tortilla Dumpling Soup, 103
 Tortilla Soup San Felipe, 102
 Turkey-Tortilla Soup, 105
Shredded Beef Enchiladas, 29
Spinach and Cheese Bake, 69
Spinach-Mushroom Pirámide, 20
Spianch-Raisin Enchiladas, 36
Spinach and Cheese Burritos, 69
Steak and Corn Tacos Picante, 52
Stir Fry Fajitas, 61
Strawberry Sherbet Cha-Cha-Cha, 118
Taco Salad Taxco, 109

Tacos:
 Chicken-Cilantro Soft Tacos ,53
 Crab Tacos with Pineapple Salsa, 54
 Flautas, 48
 Pork Tacos los Robles, 49
 Spicy Sirloin Tacos, 50
 Steak and Corn Tacos Picante, 52
 Tacos de Carne Guisada, 45
 Tacos de Frijoles y Papas, 47
 Tacos de Huachinango, 46
 Tuna Tacos with Yogurt and Mustard, 55
 Turkey-Asparagus Soft Tacos, 51
Tex-Mex Enchiladas,,37
Tortilla Bake Florentine, 22
TORTAS:
 Black Bean Tortas, 99
 Tostaditas con Guacamole, 113
TORTILLAS:
 Corn Tortillas, 123
 Flour Tortillas, 124
Tortilla Bake Florentine, 22
Tortilla-Chicken-Cheese Bake, 3
Tortilla Chips, 113
Tortilla Dumpling Soup, 103
Tortilla "Lasagne", 14
Tortilla Manicotti, 21
Tortilla Soup San Felipe, 102
Tortilla Tamale Pie, 12
TOSTADAS:
 Bacon and Egg Tostadas, 94
 Gran Tostadas Arizona, 97
 Ground Pork Tostadas, 95
 Spinach-Flank Steak Tostada, 96
 Tostadas A-Go-Go, 93
 Tostadas de Huachinango, 98
TUNA:
 Tuna Tacos with Yogurt and Mustard, 55
TURKEY:
 Curried Turkey Royale, 17
 Enchiladas de Guajolote, 30
 Quick Turkey Enchilada Casserole, 10
 Turkey-Asparagus Enchiladas Divan, 38
 Turkey-Aspoargus Soft Tacos, 51
 Turkey-Tortilla Soup, 105
 Turkey and Vegetables a la Mexicana, 8
VEGETABLES:
 Eggplant "Lasagne", 18
 Enchiladas Suizas with Spinach, 34
 Spinach and Cheese Bake, 36
 Spinach and Cheese Burritos, 69
 Spinach-Flank Steak Tostadas, 96
 Spinach-Raisin Enchiladas, 36
 Spinach-Mushroom Pirámide, 20
 Tortilla Bake Florentine, 22
Western Black Bean and Beef Bake, 19

Henry (Rick) Lorenzo, (don Enrique when he dons his Mexican apron), first discovered the intricacies of Mexican cuisine while studying at the National University of Mexico in Mexico City. He later spent many seasons at Chateau Montelén in Acapulco where he was inspired by Ramona, the talented Indian cook who reigned in the kitchen of this lovely villa. It was there that he truly learned to appreciate the versatile tortilla.

As a Spanish teacher for the Berkeley Schools, Mr. Lorenzo made sure that his students appreciated the great cuisine of Mexico. In order to successfully complete each language course, all students were required to make and share a dish using ingredients indigenous to the New World.

Mr. Lorenzo is the author of *the Berry Cookbook, the Farm Fresh Fruit Cookbook and Cookin' with Jam.*